HEROIC
LIVING

Discover *Your* Purpose *and*
Change *the* World

HEROIC
LIVING

CHRIS LOWNEY

LOYOLA PRESS.
A JESUIT MINISTRY
Chicago

LOYOLA PRESS.
A JESUIT MINISTRY

3441 N. Ashland Avenue
Chicago, Illinois 60657
(800) 621-1008
www.loyolapress.com

Unless otherwise noted, the Scripture quotations contained herein are from the New Revised Standard Version Bible: Catholic Edition, copyright ©1993 and 1989 by the Division of Christian Education of the National Council of the Churches of Christ in the U.S.A. Used by permission. All rights reserved.

Quotes from the Spiritual Exercises are from *The Spiritual Exercises of Saint Ignatius*, translation and commentary by George E. Ganss, SJ (Chicago: Loyola Press, 1992).

Cover design: Kathryn Seckman Kirsch
Cover photo: Michael Turek/GettyImages
Author photo: Michael Mella Photography
Interior design: Kathryn Seckman Kirsch and Maggie Hong

Library of Congress Cataloging-in-Publication Data
Lowney, Chris.
  Heroic living : discover your purpose and change the world / Chris Lowney.
    p. cm.
  Includes bibliographical references.
  ISBN-13: 978-0-8294-2442-3
  ISBN-10: 0-8294-2442-3
  1. Vocation—Christianity. 2. Change—Religious aspects—Christianity.
I. Title.
  BV4740.L69 2009
  248.4—dc22

                                                    2008038283

First paperback printing: August 2010
paperback ISBN–13: 978-0-8294-3295-4, ISBN–10: 0-8294-3295-7

Printed in the United States of America
        13 14 15 Bang 10 9 8 7 6 5 4 3 2

For my Mom and Dad

CONTENTS

Getting to Our Mighty Purpose. ix

Part One: Create New Strategy for a New Time

1 Our Dilemma 3
Navigate a Complex and Fast-Changing World

2 The Way Forward. 17
Create Strategy for Your Whole Life

Part Two: Discover Your Mighty Purpose

3 Where Are You Now?. 27
Evaluate the World You've Inherited

4 Where Will You Lead Us?. 39
Envision the Future Worth Fighting For

5 Why Are You Here?. 53
Articulate a Purpose Worth Living For

6 What Kind of Person Will You Be? 67
Embrace Values Worth Standing For

7 What Makes the Difference? 83
Put Heart into Strategy to Give It Life

Part Three: Choose Wisely

8 Make Great Choices 101
Learn to Use Your Head and Your Heart

9 Live in Freedom. 145
Listen to the Still, Small Voice

Part Four: Make Every Day Matter

10 Develop Consistency 157
Get the Mind-set for Getting Results

11 Recognize Progress 173
Use a Spiritual Technology for Purposeful Living

Let Gratitude and Optimism Move
You Forward. 187

Notes 195

Acknowledgments 205

Getting to
Our Mighty Purpose

You were born to change the world.

You can make the most of this unique opportunity by mastering three vital skills:

1. Articulate a purpose worth the rest of your life.
2. Make wise career and relationship choices in this changing, uncertain world.
3. Make every day matter by mindful attention to your thoughts, actions, and results.

My own improbable career—as a Jesuit seminarian and later as an investment banker—illustrates just why these particular skills are essential to a meaningful life in the twenty-first century. I was fortunate enough to serve on three continents as a managing director at J. P. Morgan & Co., which achieved the enormously ambitious goal of completely changing the company's business lines and delivering superior results while doing so. (Readers unfamiliar with business can think of it this way: we successfully overhauled and retrofitted our airplane while it was in flight—and under enemy attack). Daily life can feel similarly challenging as we teachers, lawyers, and homemakers juggle work, home, and relationships while adjusting to each day's often unwelcome surprises. The most effective of us are mastering those very skills that J. P. Morgan exemplified: understanding our strengths and weaknesses, taking control of our lives, making tough choices, and adapting as changing circumstances require.

But modern psychology informs us that healthy, happy individuals also have a deep sense of purpose. That is, they stand for cherished values, feel connected to other people, and serve causes greater than themselves and their egos. Many of us, frankly, don't find those life-giving qualities modeled in our workplaces. On the contrary, organizations can be stressful, soulless places where inauthentic managers mouth platitudes such as respect, yet treat subordinates like tools to be used and discarded. Executives articulate appealing visions, yet they lack the courage and commitment to make sacrifices for them. The worst organizations offer pay but are spiritually bankrupt, utterly incapable of providing the joy, fulfillment, or peace that we find, for example, in our families and spiritual traditions.

Many of us look to religion or spirituality for what is missing in the workplace. And though we frequently find solace and inspiration at mosque, church, or temple, we often emerge from our worship services without clear guidance for the complicated choices that the workweek will bring. Our religious traditions often provide unparalleled wisdom but no straightforward approach for weaving that wisdom through daily life. My thousand-page Bible, for all its riches, is not a strategy. Our spiritual traditions provide answers but also leave us with an increasingly vexing question: how do I connect my deepest beliefs to what I do all week at work and at home?

And so our challenge is to create a whole-life strategy that is both spiritual and worldly. Yes, we need to make tough choices, get things done, and adapt to an ever-changing world—just as the best companies do. But at the same time, we need to find peace and fulfillment by grasping the greatness that we are called to as human beings. We are here on earth to live for some mighty purpose that uplifts and stretches us. We are here to become visionaries who look beyond our self-interest and our own lifetimes, because our hearts and spirits are greater than any job or sum of money. And by transforming ourselves into who we should be, we will lead our civilization toward what it should be: not a small-spirited, self-absorbed humanity but a great-spirited civilization that loves life, other people, and the world.

What follows, then, is a how-to book for the business of being human, but it is one that rejects conventional how-to thinking. Most how-to books guarantee a result if only you read the book; this book guarantees no result if all you do is read it. Those other books typically chop our lives into pieces by focusing only on whatever problem they promise to solve—becoming a millionaire, finding a mate, getting into college, or getting a job. This book challenges us to transform work and home, beliefs and actions, body and spirit, into an integrated whole. Those books map out easy steps toward a goal; this book traces a hard path that requires lifelong practice.

The time for easy fixes is over because the easy fixes have failed. For example, too many of us are working hard but finding little satisfaction in our jobs (or, worse yet, are bored by them). Or we feel as if we are leading split lives, torn apart by competing work and family demands. A rapidly changing world bombards us with choices, and too often we choose poorly—in our relationships, careers, or lifestyles. We worry whether we will have a job tomorrow, what world our children will inherit, and, more profoundly, whether our hard work really makes much difference in this huge and complicated world. Increasing numbers of Americans report, in survey after survey, year after year, that they are mistrustful, unhappy, or unfulfilled. Half of us say that we have it worse than people did two generations ago, and 60 percent of us believe that our children will have it even worse than we do.[1]

I reject that prognosis and wrote this book out of the hopeful conviction that we can surmount the preceding afflictions, feel better about ourselves, be better versions of ourselves, and inspire our families and colleagues to be better versions of themselves, too. I know it can happen because I've seen it happen, and in the following pages we will visit family homes, the slums of Caracas, corporate boardrooms, and the garbage dumps of Manila to profile a few of the countless ordinary people who are better versions of

xii GETTING TO OUR MIGHTY PURPOSE

themselves for having found a purpose worth living for, a vision worth fighting for, and values worth standing for.

I also know that this book's strategy can work because its key practices have been working for nearly five centuries. For if the book's strategic skeleton has been influenced by J. P. Morgan (and other great organizations), its beating heart is inspired by sixteenth-century Ignatius of Loyola, founder of the Jesuit order of priests and brothers. Ignatius pioneered invaluable techniques for confronting life's fundamental questions and charting a path in response to those questions. By weaving his insights into a robust strategic framework, we will create a uniquely powerful approach to our most important business: leading our own lives.

Much (but by no means all) of this book's language will draw from the Christian tradition that I share with Ignatius of Loyola. But I'm not asking Muslim, Jewish, secular humanist, and other readers to embrace my beliefs. Instead, please ponder your own tradition's life-giving resources as you read, and I have no doubt we will all be walking a common path forward. This book's ideals are rooted in an understanding of human purpose that many great spiritual and humanistic traditions share. In fact, not my own Christian tradition, but the Tibetan Buddhism of the Dalai Lama, best summarizes the book's "case":

> If you seek enlightenment for yourself simply to enhance yourself and your position, you miss the purpose; if you seek enlightenment for yourself to enable you to serve others, you are with purpose.[2]

This century desperately needs legions more people who are willing to step up and live for a mighty purpose, who know how to make wise choices, and who can make every day matter.

PART ONE

Create New Strategy for a New Time

Navigate a complex and fast-changing world.
Create strategy for your whole life.

Discover Your Mighty Purpose

Evaluate the world you've inherited.
Envision the future worth fighting for.
Articulate a purpose worth living for.
Embrace values worth standing for.
Put heart into strategy to give it life.

Choose Wisely

Learn to use your head and your heart.
Listen to the still, small voice.

Make Every Day Matter

Get the mind-set for getting results.
Use a spiritual technology for purposeful living.

1
—

Our Dilemma

Navigate a Complex and Fast-Changing World

We modern humans absorb more information and make more decisions in an average day than our ancestors might have made in a month. Outwardly, we adapt well to this intense pace. We effortlessly transition from telephone to cell phone to instant messaging to whatever will come next. No one feels genetically urged to train carrier pigeons or to go back to using rotary-dial telephones.

But inwardly, things often go less smoothly. The multiple competing demands of daily life pull us to pieces. We work long hours to serve our families, yet in ironic consequence, we end up spending too little time with them. We make lots and lots of decisions but feel more and more stressed as we do so. We work efficiently in highly technical occupations within gigantic multinational companies, but we go home and wonder whether our work really matters.

As you read this page, four crucial factors are radically changing the landscape in which we all must live and work. Those factors are change, culture clash, increasing scale, and complexity. I'm about to tell how my onetime employer struggled to master change and complexity successfully. But this story about big business is also a parable about your life and mine. The realities that have rattled the business environment have shaken our worlds, too. In fact, we often suffer worse tremors than our employers do—because they sometimes cope with change by dumping its fallout into our laps.

Change, culture clash, increasing scale, and complexity are not going to disappear; they will accelerate. Successful organizations have been bludgeoned into understanding that a business-as-usual attitude will no longer work for them. We must realize that it won't work for us either.

Creative Destruction and an Identity Crisis

The economist Joseph Schumpeter (1883–1950) coined the term *creative destruction* to describe the displacement of existing technologies by new ones. Televisions, computers, cell phones, and automobiles are among countless twentieth-century innovations that spawned new businesses, changed our lifestyles, and enhanced our prosperity. But innovation often shapes new businesses by shattering others. Hence, Schumpeter spoke of destruction rather than evolution or transition.

Creative destruction has become even more severe since Schumpeter penned his thesis. Compare the nineteenth century to the late twentieth century. When Thomas Edison first showcased his prototype lightbulb in 1879, it was (pardon the pun) lights out for candle makers and kerosene-lamp manufacturers. But it took decades for America to be wired for electricity. Kerosene-lamp makers had time to figure out their next career moves as their sunset business slowly slid into the good night of obsolescence.

Less than a decade after Edison's lightbulb debuted, George Eastman patented the first Kodak camera, and for decades Kodak confidently hogged some 60 percent of the global film market. Company advertisements featured smiling children who reminded us to preserve our "Kodak moments." But no company executives smiled when Kodak's own moment of truth arrived with the debut of the digital camera. The new technology required no film and no chemical processing; Kodak's core businesses suddenly faced obsolescence. Film sales plummeted, and Kodak faced extinction. Candle makers had decades to outmaneuver electrification (and many of them did, judging from the extensive commerce today in candles of all shapes, sizes, and scents), but Kodak executives had months to reinvent their company. Creative destruction took a terrible toll on a company that proudly counted some 150,000 employees about two decades ago and now numbers a mere 30,000. One business reporter summed up Kodak's plight this way: "They had the brilliance to change an industry, but their hubris led them to believe that the evolution would stop with them."[1]

Kodak epitomizes the profoundly altered reality of business—and life—today. For much of their history, Kodak executives knew who they were: the world's leading manufacturer and processor of film. But today's executives live with less clarity and no long-term certainty; competitors, clients, and even core product lines can change radically over just a few years. As a result, companies and their executives must ask themselves what once would have seemed implausibly dumb questions: Who are we? What are we trying to accomplish?

Consider my own former employer, J. P. Morgan, as another example. We Morgan management trainees in 1983 knew that our key businesses were lending money to large corporations and investing their pension funds. We also knew what we didn't do: manage a retail branch network to provide mortgages and checking accounts to "ordinary" folks like you and me (I was lucky enough to be hired at J. P. Morgan, but I wasn't wealthy enough to be a customer).

Although Morgan was rated perennially America's "most admired bank," even we 1983 trainees knew that our venerable business model was doomed. Profit margins were shrinking as banks tripped over one another to lend money to big companies that enjoyed plenty of cheap fund-raising alternatives. Bankers are often portrayed as stodgy, lumbering, and change resistant; but even lumberers learn to tap-dance when change becomes imperative. Faced with grim prospects in our core business, Morgan's management launched a strategic odyssey to graft profitable, growing financial businesses onto the roots of the "old" Morgan.

To put it plainly: we were reinventing ourselves, and continuously; our businesses changed, and so did the cast of starring and supporting players. Morgan couldn't commit to businesses indefinitely, so it couldn't commit to employees indefinitely either. Businesses and employees had to "grow or go."

Some employees hunkered down fearfully, worked hard, and hoped for the best. But many others began thinking of themselves as free agents, keeping their eyes peeled for attractive job opportunities and determining never to fall in the periodic harvest of layoffs (or downsizing, rightsizing, outsourcing, or—in the ludicrous euphemism recently coined by a major U.S. company—enrollment reductions). The 1983 J. P. Morgan, in which many company veterans had long worked side by side, yielded to a workplace by the late 1990s in which lots of folks were just passing through. Of fifty or so management trainees who joined Morgan with me, not one was still with the company twenty years later.

Not only are employees passing through rapidly changing organizations, but whole companies are passing through as well. The company that today is JPMorgan Chase is an agglomeration cobbled together over the past two decades that might more accurately be called "JPMorgan-ChaseManhattan-ManufacturersHanover-ChemicalBank-BankOne-BearStearns," and so on. I've omitted a few names, but you get the idea. Marketing gurus wisely concluded that *JPMorgan Chase* fits more easily onto business cards. Like all of its competitors, JPMorgan Chase remains a work in progress that will very likely absorb new corporate DNA before this book is printed.

The companies that constitute JPMorgan Chase today were each large to begin with; now they have formed a truly colossal enterprise. In 1983 I joined a company of 20,000 or so. That seemed bewilderingly large, but it's downright puny compared to the

170,000-strong JPMorgan Chase. Today's largest companies can be likened to sizable cities: Walmart, for example, employs some two million people; that exceeds the population of Philadelphia, Detroit, or Dallas.[2]

It's easier to find a common culture and shared values in a small village than in a cosmopolitan city, and it was likewise easier to instill a J. P. Morgan way of doing things when the company was smaller and its culture so palpable that we saw and touched it—literally. I sat on the same banking floor as the illustrious J. P. Morgan Jr. himself once had; the same ornate chandelier that illuminated the titan's stern visage had brightened my desk. But today's thousands of annual hires can no longer find cultural enlightenment by meditating under the old man's chandelier and communing with his ghost; J. P. Morgan's historic banking floor, sold to real estate developers, is now a condominium lobby.

I don't recount this history out of nostalgia or bitterness. J. P. Morgan's managers very correctly realized that our old model was no longer viable, and I played my own small but certain role in consigning the good old days to the corporate dustbin. The company has continued to thrive only by doing business differently. We can think affectionately of the good old days, when the business world felt smaller, more predictable, and more manageable. But we can't linger there if we are to survive, for these stories of creative destruction serve as parables for our lives beyond the banking floor or the superstore. All of us are buffeted by the same storms that shake these companies, whether we work in a bank or in a hospital, live in a large city or out in the country, are beginning our careers or entering retirement.

We, too, must grapple with the questions that make or break big businesses today: Who are we? Why are we here? What are we trying to accomplish? Change, complexity, culture clash, and increasing scale force us to answer these fundamental questions about ourselves. And in answering them we will create the firm foundation of an enduring strategy for life.

Massive changes have affected our lives over the past decade or so: What changes—at work, in the culture, or in technology—have made an impact on yours? How is your life different today from how it was two decades ago?

Change Forces Me to
Figure Out Who I Am

Once upon a time, companies like Kodak and J. P. Morgan identified themselves with particular products (Kodak was a film manufacturer and J. P. Morgan was a moneylender). Those businesses often remained relatively stable for decades. Now companies and organizations must reinvent themselves and their businesses continually.

Once upon a time, individuals too identified themselves with a particular "product," the work they did. In fact, our ancestors' identities often literally derived from their jobs: think of surnames such as Carpenter or Baker. Mr. Baker was, well, the town baker (a profession that his son and grandson likely pursued).

But technological advances, corporate competition, and the relentless pursuit of productivity have all but obliterated the traditional career as *Webster's New World Dictionary* defines it: "a profession or occupation which one trains for and pursues as a lifework." That nice idea is thoroughly outdated for a great majority of us. Very few people nowadays will train in school for an occupation they will pursue at one company throughout their working lifetime. Instead, it's estimated that today's college graduates will typically work for some seven to ten different employers during a career. I know people who have cycled through ten different companies by the age of thirty.

Most of us will live decades longer than our great-grandparents did and will grow old in a world unrecognizably different from the one into which we were born. Many adults have already lived through the advent of televisions, cell phones, personal computers, and jet travel. And anyone who dares predict the technological landscape of 2050 will likely be as far off base as the nineteenth-century U.S. Patent Office commissioner who is said to have predicted that "Everything that can be invented has been invented."[3]

A relentlessly changing world forces us not only to adapt and be flexible but also to confront fundamental questions about our identity. One of our great-grandparents might have said, "I am Mr. Baker, the town baker." But a job never has captured the fullness of a person's identity. That is especially true now that most of us will pursue multiple jobs and enjoy many further productive years once our working careers end. Not only does it make little sense to derive our identity chiefly from a job, but also it is no longer possible to do so, given all the changes that shape our work life.

When careers were more stable, life's key question seemed to be, What job will I do? Now the key questions are more profound and more challenging: Who am I? Why am I here on earth? What kind of person will I be? I may do lots of jobs during a career, but as I move from one job to another—even from one company or profession to another—what remains? I remain. Who is that person, and what is he or she living for, beyond the next paycheck? If I can't consciously articulate some overall, unifying meaning to my life, then my life ends up as a series of disconnected episodes as I drift between jobs, through relationships, and into retirement.

Culture Clash Forces Me to Figure Out What I Stand For

As companies and individuals navigate change, conflicts arise about how work should be done and how life should be lived. I was privileged, for example, to live and work on three continents, which put me center stage for sometimes trivial and sometimes profound cultural clashes. We Americans thought we knew how business ought to be conducted: internal meetings in New York were freewheeling affairs in which everyone from lowly trainees to managing directors frankly disputed the merits of various proposals. Client meetings quickly came to the point as we pitched business transactions and all but bullied our clients into awarding us deals.

But when we Americans disembarked airplanes in Japan, our certainties evaporated. We couldn't figure out whether to bow to Japanese colleagues or shake their hands, or both. We strode into business meetings and pitched aggressively for deals, leaving our Japanese colleagues and clients a bit embarrassed and appalled by our forwardness and seeming insensitivity to the building of long-term relationships.

Life in this global era has dunked us into a wonderfully refreshing yet maddeningly diverse cultural pool. We speak numerous languages and eat from a variety of cuisines. Many of us believe in God, and many of us don't. Some of us won't have sex before marriage, and others will "hook up" after exchanging a few e-mails. My grandparents passed virtually their whole lives in one town among familiar neighbors who shared a common worldview and values. In contrast, I often brush by as many people in one day as they met in a lifetime. The common worldview of their small village has yielded to my cosmopolitan cacophony of religious, ethnic, generational, and other cultures.

Change forced us to ask, Who am I? Why am I here on earth? Cultural diversity adds other fundamental questions to our growing list: How should I behave and treat other people? What values are important and fundamental, in business and in personal life?

In a homogenous, stable culture, we often absorbed the answers from home, school, and neighborhood—and mostly we took the answers for granted. Now we must consciously ask and answer those questions for ourselves.

Scale Forces Me to Consider Why I Matter

We face other life-defining questions thanks to another modern phenomenon: companies that have become gigantic in a world that's shrinking.

Modern media bombard us with news and images from an ever-smaller world: we watch in real time as Britons escape buses shattered by terrorist bombings while we simultaneously send instant messages to our business acquaintances there to confirm their safety. Yet, as the world becomes smaller, we often feel smaller, too. Every night we see earth-shaping events in faraway places that might affect our own safety and livelihoods; yet we feel powerless to do much about any of it—or we switch the channel to lighter fare, only to be reminded that our humdrum, work-and-come-home lives pale beside the apparently rich, full lives of celebrities.

The galloping gigantism of modern commerce further compounds the impression that we are relatively insignificant cogs in the world's large-scale machinery. My grandfather, basically a subsistence farmer, could see face-to-face the good he accomplished. He lived among the growing children he nourished; he helped build the house that sheltered them.

I, too, helped to feed and shelter people. J. P. Morgan financed and advised supermarket chains, home builders, and food manufacturers; our company employed thousands of people, enabling them to support their families with dignity; we managed pension funds that ensured countless retirees a stable, comfortable old age. My J. P. Morgan colleagues and I helped feed and shelter more people than either my late grandfather or I could possibly imagine.

That's just the problem: I couldn't imagine. Big can be beautiful for the efficiency and expertise that result when humans join together to embrace common goals on a great scale. But big can be demoralizing when bankers, accountants, administrative assistants, and human-resource professionals search for meaning in our work. My grandfather's generation, most of whom were self-employed in small shops or farms, often knew and interacted with the people they fed. Employees in my generation, often moored to workstations in a sea of cubicles, watch numbers on spreadsheets, not families eating the food we grow. We can feel alienated—cut off— from the products our employers produce and from the humans they serve. We service loans that finance factories we never visit; the factories bake bread destined for nameless towns strung across the continent.

We know our work must make a difference, yet it's sometimes impossible to discern just what that difference is. Even if I heroically shouldered the workload of two people—and sometimes I did—it neither lowered the cost of J. P. Morgan's services by a penny nor raised the company's earnings per share by a penny. How discouraging! When I left Morgan, someone replaced me, and business hummed along as business always had. Indeed, so many colleagues came and went that it became ever harder to find community at work; we rode elevators alongside nearly anonymous colleagues who spun through the company's revolving doors each day, all of them segmented into specialized departments that were scattered all over J. P. Morgan's worldwide network.

Scale and its by-products, such as highly specialized occupations, can leave us feeling alienated, insignificant, and isolated. In 1800, four out of five people were self-employed and thus quite connected to the people affected by their labor.[4] Our connection to work is very different now. Hence, further questions accumulate on our growing list: Why do I matter? What makes my life meaningful?

Put differently, giant-sized companies can often offer pay but not meaning. Increasingly, we must find meaning for ourselves.

What principles do you follow in dealing with other people?

Are they rules you learned growing up, in church, in your profes-sional life?

What makes life deeply meaningful for you? Why is it important that you are here in this world of six billion people?

Complexity Forces Me to Figure Out How to Make Good Choices

The three trends just discussed—change, clashing cultures, and scale—are conspiring with a host of others to render contemporary life enormously complex. We enjoy vastly more work and lifestyle options than our grandparents did. But more options translate into more decisions we must make. We choose whether or not to attend college, which college to attend, what job to pursue, where to live, whom to marry, when to switch jobs, and how much to save for retirement. In fact, we will make some of those choices multiple times during our long working life before deciding when to retire. And let's not forgot life's more mundane choices, such as which of some one hundred brands of breakfast cereal to buy.

You would think that all of that decision making would turn us into astute decision makers. But evidence suggests the opposite. Researchers have discovered, for example, that whether it's 401(k) investment choices or brands of jam in a supermarket, humans tend to choose most conscientiously and wisely when weighing only a limited number of variables. We become bewildered by large arrays of choices and intimidated by the complexity of sorting through them. So, we go with our gut, mimic a friend's choices, or play Eeny Meeny Miney Mo.

In other words, the sheer number of choices we have to make—along with the complexity of those choices—has eroded our ability to make those choices well. And sometimes Eeny Meeny Miney Mo seems as good an alternative as any, given the tough choices that often confront us. We face seemingly irreconcilable trade-offs, like having to decide (under time pressure, of course) between a job transfer that will benefit our career but that may hurt our family life. Or, worse yet, we don't feel sufficient control over our circumstances to make good choices, like countless folks who cling to unfulfilling jobs to retain benefits that they don't want to risk forfeiting.[5]

A New World Approach to New World Realities

A list of uncomfortable questions has piled up throughout this chapter:

- Who am I?
- What am I trying to accomplish in life?
- How should I behave and treat other people?
- What values are important and fundamental, in business and in family life?
- Why do I matter?
- What makes my life meaningful?

In the ancient world of, say, twenty years ago, we could skip these philosophical questions and get right to the nitty-gritty ones, such as where to work and live. But change, culture clash, scale, and complexity won't allow us to operate in that old-fashioned way any longer. Before we are bankers, priests, astronauts, or film manufacturers, we are human beings. So the first and most strategic question we must ask is, What does it mean to be a fulfilled, purposeful, successful human being?

If we don't tackle the question of what makes human life meaningful, we may end up becoming expert and successful in ways that we'll discover, late in life, were not very meaningful at all. Before worrying about what we're doing for a living, we need to figure out what we're living for, because our "career" in the environment of the new world is not a job. It is our whole life.

So how do we go about answering the big questions? And how do we translate our answers into good choices in life and effective day-to-day performance? We do so by engaging this complex, changing world in a much more deliberate, proactive, and purposeful manner. We need a new approach to the business of living. We need a strategy.

2
—

The Way Forward
Create Strategy for Your Whole Life

In 2001, Gerald Levin, chief executive of the goliath Time Warner magazine and cable television conglomerate, engineered a merger with AOL that profoundly shook the business world by marrying traditional media with new Internet media. Investors later second-guessed that move, but none doubted that he had pursued a bold direction for Time Warner. As Internet commerce began exploding, so did the assumptions and business models that had long guided companies like Time Warner. Levin and his management colleagues had responded by charting a fresh strategy.

Ironically, although Mr. Levin was creating a strategy for Time Warner's business, he didn't seem to have a strategy for his most important business: his own life. Here is how he described himself, some years after the merger: "I woke up one day at age sixty-three and I didn't know anything about the most fundamental questions of life." That self-revelation led to a resolution: "I'm going on a journey. I'm going to find myself."[1]

The moral of the story? Neither our companies nor we as individuals can improvise our way through life. And we're not going to navigate the twenty-first-century landscape with the equivalent of nineteenth-century compasses. We need a deliberately crafted way forward, a strategy. Without one, we run the risk that, like Levin, we might wake up one day, confront life's "fundamental questions," and wonder why we've lived as we have.

Strategy is a fancy-sounding word for a very straightforward concept, and Levin's metaphor of a journey helps us grasp the essence of good strategy. Yes, we are on a journey through life. Only fools will wander aimlessly on that journey, or stride off in one direction without knowing where they are trying to go, or change course to follow every passing crowd, or start their journey without gathering some of the tools and resources they will need along the way. Wise people figure out where they want to go and gather the tools they need to get there.

The metaphor may sound too simple. Surely a sophisticated-sounding concept like strategy must entail a far more complex process. Yet the Harvard Business School professor Michael Porter, perhaps America's foremost academic in the field of corporate strategy, defines strategy just that simply: "a combination of the ends (goals) for which the firm is striving and the means (policies) by which it is seeking to get there."[2] More plainly: figure out where you want to go and identify the tools and resources to get there.

Our Way through the Chapters Ahead

Any good strategy, therefore, deals first with ends (purpose or life direction) and then with means (tools, tactics, and resources). With this idea of strategy in mind, we will reflect intensely in coming chapters on our human purpose and then develop two essential tools for attaining it. In part 2, we will think about purpose by dealing with very fundamental questions. We will take stock of the world we've inherited (chapter 3) and decide what kind of world we will help create (chapter 4). We will articulate our "mighty purpose" (chapter 5) and decide what values we will stand for throughout our earthly journey (chapter 6). Throughout the process we will begin to build a strategy big enough and meaningful enough to last a lifetime. But we will also face the reality that good strategy is not a sterile head game (chapter 7); we need heart and soul to bring strategy alive.

In part 3, we'll start focusing on the means to achieve a mighty purpose: we'll learn how to make major decisions. It's one thing to figure out what our lifelong purpose is; it's quite another to figure out whether to live that purpose as a priest or a dentist, whether and whom to marry, or what lifestyle choices to make while in school, a career, or retirement. We bring purpose to life by making decisions, so one critical factor in our strategy must be a process for making life's big choices.

In part 4, we'll tackle implementation, because once we make choices, we must live them out, day after day. We'll add some critical tools for getting things done and assessing our progress, every day of our lives, so that we can make every day matter. It's what one best-selling business guide refers to as, "execution—the discipline of getting things done."[3]

Discover a mighty purpose . . . Choose wisely . . . Make every day matter. Our strategy will proceed from the very big picture (why are we humans here on earth?) to the very small picture (how can I be more productive this afternoon than I was this morning?). That's a breathtaking sweep, encompassing everything from why I exist, to whether I should be a doctor, to how I can more effectively work with my patients today. But a good strategy must trace a breathtaking sweep: when we compartmentalize life—for example, by separating work life from home life or what we believe from what we do—we are often left with a mess that doesn't quite hang together as an integrated whole.

Our strategy is not going to be a plan we will write but the way we will live. It's not about filling out questionnaires and manipulating spreadsheets to produce an imposing document that will gather dust on a shelf. Rather, it's about developing skills—such as decision making and daily updating—that we will practice for the rest of our lives and sharpen as we go along.

This strategy will remain as relevant at age sixty-three as it is at eighteen, and whether starting a first career or a fourth one. Some readers might not see it that way. They are doing fine, have good jobs, and are raising children successfully; or, they are happy, popular, doing well in school, and enjoy promising job prospects. Well, Gerald Levin could have boasted such attainments as well, but those successes, though important, are only pieces of a larger puzzle. Finding a well-paying job is not the same as addressing what Levin called "the fundamental questions" of life. His career is exhibit 1. He reached the pinnacle of American commerce.

But he later confronted questions that he apparently had skipped during his rise. Yes, he may have made the most of his career, but he wasn't sure whether he had made the most of his life. The Greek sage Aristotle put it this way: "If, like archers, we have a target to aim at, we are more likely to hit the right mark."[4] Aristotle wasn't talking about shorter-term targets, such as getting a great job or becoming a millionaire, but about the more fundamental concern of what a well-lived, purposeful life entails. That fundamental concern comes first.

More than two millennia later, another great sage warned that we seem to be forgetting Aristotle's wisdom. As Albert Einstein put it, "Perfection of means and confusion of ends seems to characterize our age."[5] In other words, as a society we race after new technologies, weaponry, gadgets, and fads without pausing to ponder whether they will serve us well in the long run. And, as individuals, we fixate on how to get jobs, get mates, or get rich without first contemplating our human end, as Aristotle put it, or life's fundamental questions, as Levin phrased it.

We need to avoid the trap that Einstein so aptly described. Of course we all want to resolve today's most pressing concern, like whether to marry this person or how to get a better-paying job. But we can't adequately address those day-to-day concerns until we've taken care of lifelong ones; we can't focus on the means and neglect the ends.

As Levin's story illustrates, we fall into a trap when we subconsciously begin to equate our purpose in life with a job—or with any other activities that happen to fill our days. That makes for a very impoverished idea of purpose. Let's not sell ourselves so short—we are greater than our jobs! In the following chapters we'll try to articulate some sense of purpose that will be powerful enough to lift us above our everyday concerns and expansive enough to last a lifetime. As a result, our strategy is going to delve deeply into the questions that many self-help guides skip, those same questions that piled up throughout the previous chapter: What is my purpose? What makes life meaningful? How should we treat other people? And, most vexingly, Can I manage to connect my deepest beliefs about meaning and purpose to the everyday choices I make in life and business?

Enter the *Spiritual Exercises* of Ignatius Loyola

St. Ignatius of Loyola founded the Society of Jesus (the Jesuits) during the sixteenth century. At first glance, his masterwork, the *Spiritual Exercises*, hardly looks like a strategy guide. The exercises are a series of meditations on the life and mission of Jesus Christ. They include, for example, a meditation on hell and a contemplation to attain love, hardly things a business guru would expect to find in a strategy document.

But for nearly five centuries, these exercises have remained one of humanity's more powerful instruments for confronting life's fundamental questions and figuring out one's path in response. One of Europe's brightest Renaissance intellectuals, for example, said after completing them, "I am completely invigorated and seem to be changed into an entirely new man." And today, centuries later, thousands of corporate executives, retirees, high school students, alcoholics, and others are engaging in these exercises all over the world with similarly powerful results.

Once we wade past their arcane language, it becomes apparent that the exercises treat the very same concerns outlined in this book thus far. For example, we're interested in developing techniques for making good choices, and Ignatius offers intriguing approaches that will round out any parent's or businessperson's decision-making tool kit. Likewise, where we are concerned about implementing choices well on a daily basis, Ignatius suggests a handy process for doing so.

By linking Ignatius's spiritual insights and modern ideas about strategy, we will create something unique and uniquely powerful: neither the Spiritual Exercises nor a stereotypical business-style strategy, but an approach to living that taps into great insights from both. We will chart a way of living and working that is both worldly and spiritual, that helps us connect our deepest beliefs to what we do all day. Instead of trapping ourselves in a split life with compartmentalized thinking, we'll free ourselves by pursuing a whole-life strategy.

This whole-life strategy will be easier to outline than to internalize. Our culture of instant gratification, unfortunately, has beguiled us into imagining otherwise: that we can bring about profound personal transformation, for example, during a short airline flight by flipping through a how-to book even as we are shuffling through musical selections on a personal music player.

Every great spiritual tradition reminds us that we need to make an investment to get a result. Serious Buddhists, for example, devote countless hours to their meditative practices and understand that there are no shortcuts. And great humanistic traditions do likewise: members of Alcoholics Anonymous speak frequently of "working the steps," that is, investing the substantial reflective time required to process the twelve introspective steps of the AA program.

So Ignatius advises anyone who "desires to make all the progress possible" to "withdraw [temporarily] from all friends and acquaintances, and from all earthly concerns; for example, by moving out of one's place of residence and taking a different house or room where one can live in the greatest possible solitude" (#20).

That was a radical proposal even in the sixteenth century; it's even more bracing nowadays. After stressful days surfing tides of e-mail, phone calls, meetings, and distractions, we unwind by tethering ourselves to cell phones, portable music players, or other gadgets that insulate us from our inner selves. We've grown ever more adept at manipulating video remotes through hundreds of cable channels and ever less adept at tuning into ourselves. As individuals—and as a culture—we are losing the time, inclination, and skill to focus introspectively.

Most strategies for change (whether prescriptions for personal growth or formulas for organizational change and leadership) don't really work because they remain sterile head games or quick-fix concoctions of checklists and surefire solutions. Instead of memorizing handy checklists, we need to spend time alone with ourselves, face the facts about ourselves, and compare our present reality to our deepest beliefs and aspirations about who we should be and what we want our world to be.

The following chapters will profile a handful of people who have done just that and who are finding great purpose in their very ordinary roles as teachers, parents, maintenance workers, lawyers, and so on. None of them is famous, which is exactly the point. Our culture has come to associate great purpose only with history-shaping moguls and luminaries strutting across the world stage. We've confused great purpose with great deeds and associated heroism with fame: how can my father, boss, teacher, or daughter be a hero unless the newspapers or television have said so?

Let's recover the true meaning and nature of heroism. Dictionaries define *hero* not by how widely celebrated a person is, but by the qualities he or she exemplifies, such as strength, courage, and nobility.

The heroes introduced in the following chapters fit that definition but buck the hero-celebrity stereotype. They aren't recognizable names, but they do embody strength, courage, or nobility that make them worthy human ideals. Their heroism springs not from game-winning touchdown passes or war victories but from humble, simple acts like changing a diaper, polishing a floor, or perfecting a spreadsheet. These humbler heroes challenge us not to look at them in wonder but to look at ourselves and find similarly great purpose and meaning in our own life and work. Can we see our own mundane routines as opportunities to exemplify timeless values? Can we believe that even while worrying about next week's work deadline we can pursue a vision that transcends our whole lifetime? Can we be bold enough to believe that we are doing extraordinary things even in the most ordinary gestures of our lives as parents, teachers, and bankers?

The following chapters invite us not only to articulate this greater vision of ourselves but also to discover a turning point that might yield the courage and commitment to become that greater vision of ourselves. Some may realize that living for a mighty purpose will require a fundamental change in how they are living or in the live-lihoods they are pursuing. But many—most of us, I suspect—will come to realize that we've been quietly living a profound purpose all along. We've only lacked the vision to see the profound impor-tance of what we do all day, the words to capture the noble values our lives have been about, and the courage of our convictions to stand confidently for those values in a world that may consider us foolish or naive.

The following chapter begins the journey to clearer purpose. But before we launch any journey, we need to understand something basic: where are we starting from, and how did we get here? We turn to those questions first.

What would you consider the fundamental questions of life? Have you asked and answered them for yourself?

What tools or technologies do you typically use when you face a major decision, such as a career change? Do you have a consis-tent approach or take each decision as it comes?

Create New Strategy for a New Time
Navigate a complex and fast-changing world.
Create strategy for your whole life.

PART TWO

Discover Your Mighty Purpose

Evaluate the world you've inherited.
Envision the future worth fighting for.
Articulate a purpose worth living for.
Embrace values worth standing for.
Put heart into strategy to give it life.

Choose Wisely
Learn to use your head and your heart.
Listen to the still, small voice.

Make Every Day Matter
Get the mind-set for getting results.
Use a spiritual technology for purposeful living.

Discover Your Mighty Purpose
» Evaluate the world you've inherited.
Envision the future worth fighting for.
Articulate a purpose worth living for.
Embrace values worth standing for.
Put heart into strategy to give it life.

3

Where Are You Now?
Evaluate the World You've Inherited

Ignatius Loyola's Spiritual Exercises invite us to look at the world as God would see it: "full of people . . . so diverse in dress and behavior: some white and others black, some in peace and others at war, some weeping and others laughing, some healthy and others sick, some being born and others dying" (#102, #106). What would God think of the state of our world? What do you think of it?

Why is this mental exercise important? Because facing facts about the world right now can help us see more clearly how we want to lead our civilization forward. What kind of world are we living in, where is it heading, and what part has each of us played in getting it there? Those big-picture questions typically remain unanswered because so many other concerns tunnel our vision. No future world event seems more consequential than the size of my upcoming raise, and no past injustice seems greater than the money I lost to the coffee vendor who shortchanged me this morning. For an accurate perception of our world, we have to lift our heads a bit higher in order to see a bit farther. We do this by taking what an early guidebook to the *Spiritual Exercises* called "a global view of all the world in its variety and woes."[1]

It's difficult to form an accurate global view of a complex world from our humble human perch, and even some of history's greatest

minds have stumbled spectacularly while trying to do so. For example, during the sixth century, Pope Gregory the Great moaned,
"The world grows old and hoary and hastens to approaching death."[2]
A full millennium later, in the eighteenth century, the equally pes-
simistic British sage Robert Malthus postulated that the planet was
crowded with about as many people as it could possibly feed. He
foresaw a harrowing cycle: famine, plague, and poverty would periodically winnow the overtaxed planet of its weakest; then population would climb for a while until the horrible cycle erupted anew
to purge a once-again overburdened globe.

That was about 6 billion people ago. Malthus scanned a British
countryside where farmers loosened poorly irrigated earth with crude
picks and hoes, never imagining that today's farmers would pilot
air-conditioned, global positioning system–guided tractors across
vast expanses of well-irrigated farmland that burgeon with ever-
hardier crop strains to feed an ever-healthier populace. Premature
babies who would have been given up for dead in Malthus's day are
now nursed to a healthy infancy; vaccines shield them from polio,
measles, and other crippling diseases. And once these infants reach
their golden years, artificial hips, transplanted hearts, and an arsenal of medicines ward off the ravages of old age.

We Americans enjoy nearly twice the average life expectancy of
our great-grandparents and immeasurably higher living standards.
Twice as many of us graduate from high school; almost all of us are
literate. Once upon a time most of us worked on family farms; now
most of us choose among countless occupations and pastimes.

And as if there aren't enough choices already, an ever-evolving
economy spawns completely new professions annually as we, like
our Creator, make the world not only life giving and sustaining
but also beautiful and interesting. God didn't rest after providing
life's mere necessities, such as arable land and oxen to drag plows
through it. Rather, God also created fanciful sunsets, rainbows, and
sandy beaches. And we, God's cocreators, have likewise invented
and discovered not only what nourishes and sustains life but also
what makes it more beautiful, fun, interesting, and entertaining.

We've created baseball and curling, opera and jazz, the Slinky and Etch A Sketch, the *Iliad* and *Harry Potter*, and architectural gems that both resist earthquakes and please the eye.

This millennia-long riot of healing, nurturing, nourishing, and creating has generated such incredible prosperity that average Americans in the late twentieth century managed to live more comfortably than did the nineteenth-century's wealthiest tycoons. Take, for example, J. Pierpont Morgan, who founded the company I worked for. He owned a more luxurious yacht than I will ever afford, but jets transport me to more places annually than Morgan visited in his lifetime (even if I get there in a cramped seat with only pretzels for sustenance). Morgan bought priceless manuscripts and ancient artifacts; but he never watched a television, browsed a Web site, or looked at a color photograph. And if I were afflicted by the same unsightly, bulbous nose that marred the wealthy Morgan's physique, I could buy what no amount of his nineteenth-century wealth could have afforded: a nose job.

Such are the miracles of progress. Morgan's contemporary Andrew Carnegie put it succinctly: "The poor enjoy what the rich could not before afford."[3] All in all, when I "gaze upon the whole circuit of the world," as Ignatius counsels, I'm quite happy to be one of those billions who today defy Malthus's pessimism. I'm grateful to my ancestors. I'm grateful to each generation's parents, who nurse and nourish the billions of us, and to the teachers who taught us to read, and to the neighbors who look after us in playgrounds, and to the businesspeople who create opportunities for us to exercise our talents and support our families with dignity, and to the public servants who work conscientiously to keep our communities healthy and safe. To paraphrase Sir Isaac Newton, we lead longer, healthier, and more prosperous lives because we stand on the shoulders of giants. Indeed, as I think of all I have and all I have been given, I'm certain of this much: I haven't been grateful enough—and, chances are, neither have you.

Be grateful now, tomorrow, every morning, and every evening. We have so much, and we've come so far. In the chapters to come, we are called to embrace some mighty purpose. But as the Roman orator Cicero reminded us, "For Gratitude not merely stands alone at the head of all the virtues, but is even mother of all the rest."[4] Whatever purpose we embrace in life, we'll do so more productively and effectively when filled with gratitude for all that we have and for all that we have to offer.

We've Come So Far, but Where Are We Going?

Yet doubts intrude as I face the facts about where we humans have gotten ourselves. For starters, why aren't more of us happier? The same Carnegie who celebrated progress also lamented, "The price we pay for this salutary change is, no doubt, great."[5] Today's average American may be twice as prosperous as his or her grandparents, yet fewer of us now report that we are "very happy"; four times as many of us say we are lonely.[6] We trust one another less; fewer than 10 percent of us feel that the integrity and honesty of the average American is improving, and two-thirds of us believe that moral values have been deteriorating in the United States.[7] Those statistics don't sound very optimistic because we're not optimistic: 66 percent of us think that our children will have it worse than we do.[8]

We're healthier and wealthier than any civilization in human history, but we're vaguely dissatisfied and chasing something that always tantalizingly eludes us. When asked, for example, how much annual income they would need to "live well," Americans at virtually every income level answer, "Twice as much."[9] The person earning $50,000 annually believes he or she needs $100,000 to live well, and those making $200,000 believe they need $400,000.

As a former investment banker who worked alongside the planet's best-paid people, I've been jarred to see disconsolate multimillionaires in tears about their paychecks. A partner at a rival bank once described the attitude among hotshot bankers who receive annual bonus checks that sometimes exceed an average American's lifetime earnings: "They are either sullen or mutinous," the ex-partner described, "but never quite happy."[10]

The sullen protest that it "isn't about the money," and often it isn't. It's about what they might call respect, or fairness, or keeping score, or recognition, or having power, or being the best, or being number one. Yet money seldom buys those things either, as the very wealthiest continuously discover. As a multimillionaire founder of a technology company once confessed to a reporter, "There's an A-list here, and then there's everyone else. And I'm not A-list."[11] The first-century Jewish sage Rabbi Meir summed up our twenty-first-century predicament: "Who is wealthy? One who derives inner peace from his fortune."[12]

Amen, Rabbi Meir. We're financially better off, yet we're not better off at all, are we? The middle class envy the wealthy, while the wealthy envy the superwealthy. We're all chasing something, yet we're never quite attaining it. Disturbingly, we've apparently been at this chase for longer than two centuries. Here's how Alexis de Tocqueville described it in the late 1700s: "[Americans] find prosperity almost everywhere, but not happiness. For the desire for well-being has become a restless burning passion which increases with satisfaction."[13]

So we turn in other directions to satisfy our restless, insatiable passions. We are eating ourselves to death; the percentage of obese Americans has nearly doubled in the past fifteen years.[14] And we are eating our planet to death. Average-sized houses have grown twice as large in only one generation, and in order to build and equip them, we consume natural resources at irreplaceable rates.[15] Then we fill the resulting craters with plastic bags, beer cans, and whatever other junk we've discarded after temporarily quenching one or another of our bottomless appetites. The luxurious personal universe we're trying to create for ourselves may leave only a rav-aged, junk-strewn, overly indebted one to our grandchildren.

Still, we don't find what we desire. Maybe we're looking in the wrong places? That's what self-described "beauty junkie" Alex Kuczynski, concluded after enduring some sixteen eyelid lifts (and assorted other plastic surgeries) before she admitted to herself that the seventeenth wouldn't be the one that brought her to her "ultimate goal: happiness and satisfaction." [16]

The progress of progress has deluded our civilization into imagining that all our problems will be solved by, well, more material progress. After all, gross national product and living standards inexorably rise generation after generation. Yet fulfillment, satisfaction, peace, and joy have not been rising in the same proportions. In fact, they have been stagnating.

We in the developed world have failed to make ourselves any happier or more fulfilled than we were decades ago. We don't have the satisfaction we crave, yet we are too shortsighted to notice that the road we're traveling won't get us there. Once we lift our heads high enough to take in a bird's-eye view of our culture, we, the world's prosperous, start to seem like a convoy of anxious drivers lost together on a foggy road, carrying on and hoping we'll soon pop out into sunshine. Unfortunately, we're not driving toward fulfillment; we're driving ourselves nuts.

We need to face the facts about our wrongheaded culture not only for our own sakes but also because our beloved children and grandchildren are now eagerly following us on the fast lane to not-quite-where-we-want-to-go. In a recent Pew Research Center survey, 81 percent of eighteen- to twenty-five-year-olds said that getting rich is either their generation's most important life goal or its second most important goal, and 51 percent of them said the same thing about getting famous. [17]

We also need to face the facts because, while we in the United States are racing hard on our misdirected quest, our brothers and sisters in the developing world are racing hard, too. But the planet's most impoverished are running not to get rich but simply to outrace hunger, disease, and abject poverty. Nearly 2 billion of them scratch out miserable livelihoods on less than $2 a day. They don't wonder why a larger house or fancier car isn't making them happy; they worry about scraping together a meal for their children today.

I've visited a few of these brothers and sisters of ours, some of them on the outskirts of Manila, in the Philippines, at the foot of a garbage dump that sprawled as far as I could see. Some seventy thousand people live in and around this "town's" sixty-four thousand acres. The heart of what we might uncharitably but accurately call Garbage Kingdom is a garbage mountain that swarms daily with men, women, and young children attired not in protective hazmat uniforms but in T-shirts, shorts, and flip-flops. These prospectors pay the municipal government a few cents for the privilege of scampering up the garbage hillside; they earn back their up-front investment by selling plastics, metals, and other valuables scavenged by overturning layer upon layer of Manila's refuse. Free market economists would be appalled by the work but would admire the compensation system: pay for productivity and no free ride for underperformers.

The Garbage Kingdom's treasures are constantly replenished. The city of Manila is 11 million strong, and its citizens generate lots of trash. Trucks rumble along every few minutes to tip a new mother lode onto the pile. Enterprising pickers crowd in, as if ducking under a waterfall—to my eyes it is a trashfall of every rotten leftover ever thrown in a garbage pail; to theirs it is a cascade of money. The most valuable trash is invariably snapped up as soon as it hits the pile, and some Garbage Kingdom prospectors pay extra to stand beside the unloading trucks.

Young children also scamper across Garbage Kingdom. Shorter and nimbler than their parents, the children stoop to comb through garbage without suffering the spine-wearying back pain that afflicts both wealthy adult gardeners and impoverished trash prospectors. The children seem to actually enjoy the work. Besides, what else would their parents do with them? Garbage pickers can't afford nannies or day care. And these little children, blessed with small hands, keen eyesight, and boundless energy, are often more talented pickers than their parents. How deeply it must assault a parent's dignity not only to pick garbage for a living and to drag his or her children into the business but also to realize that they are more effective trash-picking breadwinners.

At the foot of Garbage Kingdom stands, quite incongruously, a small house with an adjacent wading pool. Its proprietors are two nuns who mind some of Garbage Kingdom's children every afternoon. These children may be wonderful garbage pickers, but diminishing marginal returns (as economists would put it) eventually set in. Little children grow hungry and cranky after working under the Manila sun in temperatures that hover around 100 degrees Fahrenheit. So the nuns take the children off their parents' hands each afternoon, feed them, play games, and teach them to read. And the wading pool? No child likes to wash, whether living in luxury or in Garbage Kingdom. But every child likes to splash around after a hot morning in the sun. The sisters use the wading pool to trick the children into bathing.

Some of these children will eventually attend primary school. Others will enter the family business in Garbage Kingdom. Frankly, the job pays better than many others in a country that offers too few jobs in the first place.

This can't possibly be the way humans are supposed to live, by God's plan or anyone else's. Yet I jetted home from Garbage Kingdom to New York, washed away a long trip's grime and slept away its jet lag, and never did much about what I saw. What could I have done really? Send money, I suppose, but I worry about the corruption and inefficiency that hobble so many humanitarian efforts. Besides, so many needy causes beckon, even in my home country, that it's hard to know which ones to support. I worry, too, about my own future: how much can I set aside for Garbage Kingdom without endangering my long-term security? After all, an unexpected stock market decline or serious illness could drastically diminish my savings. Life is complicated, it's too difficult to sort through all the variables, daily life's fast-flowing river soon pulls me back into the downstream current, and Garbage Kingdom slowly recedes from view.

For a short while, Garbage Kingdom loomed in front of me, swarming with my impoverished brothers and sisters, and there seemed no way around it. But over time Garbage Kingdom faded into the distance and became a barely perceptible blip on the horizon. New problems and opportunities emerged to push old ones from my consciousness.

When you take a bird's-eye view of the world, what makes you grateful? What problems and heartbreaks do you see?

Good Strategists Face the Facts

Every good strategy begins with facing the facts about ourselves and the world around us. This chapter has, in an abbreviated way, "gaze[d] upon the whole circuit of the world," as Ignatius of Loyola would put it. We see a civilization that has grown immensely more prosperous. Yet many who prosper haven't found the personal satisfaction and fulfillment that they crave above all. And while we prosper, millions of our brothers and sisters crawl around garbage dumps in Manila, or die of AIDS in South Africa, or scrape by on $2 a day, or suffer illiteracy and its burdens.

What are we to make of these facts? We see three unfolding crises: the search for fulfillment in the prosperous world, the misery of the developing world's poor, and the mounting anxiety of those stuck in the middle. These three crises are related, all consequences of a culture slowly veering off track. We are losing our way.

Prosperity itself isn't the problem. It's a blessing—we Americans are better educated than our great-grandparents, and we live longer, healthier lives. But without the continuous march forward of prosperity, children will still be scrambling around Manila garbage dumps generations from now.

But prosperity and wealth are merely a means to more dignified, fulfilled lives; they are not the end purpose of life itself. As Einstein observed, "perfection of means" and "confusion of ends" aptly describe our age. Prosperity should be serving us; instead, we have become slaves to prosperity. We labor through ever-longer work-weeks, worry about whether we are falling behind the neighbors, and see the superrich pulling farther and farther ahead of us—and even as the superrich continue to accumulate money, power, stuff, and status, our exhausting, self-absorbed strategy has made us no happier than we were two generations ago. As greed (and its cousins, pride and obsession with ego) increasingly grip our culture, our desire for more prosperity becomes, as Tocqueville put it, a "restless, burning passion which [only] increases with satisfaction."[18]

Those at the bottom of humanity's material heap, in Manila garbage dumps and elsewhere, suffer most from this misguided culture that worships the rich and famous instead of those who have bettered the lives of the world's garbage pickers, homeless, refugees, illiterate, or jobless. We are considered successful when we compare favorably to our neighbors, not when we contribute to their well-being. We're turning into, as pundits have dubbed it, the YOYO society, that is, "You're on your own." You're on your own, my forlorn garbage-picking friend; good luck with your struggles.

Those stuck in the middle also suffer. We live far more comfortably than our great-grandparents could have dreamed. But the YOYO society affords only a precarious fingerhold on prosperity—we worry about saving enough to support ourselves in old age or to educate our children. A neighbor loses his job, and we shudder to think how quickly our own comfortable lifestyle could crumble: we are a paycheck away from lost health insurance, late mortgage payments, and the threat of financial catastrophe. We live amid uncertainty, and neither working harder nor praying harder will bring the security we crave. So we in the middle sometimes envy the wealthy, which only compounds our anxiety with unhappiness. Or we might imitate the acquisitive lifestyles of the wealthy, choosing to compete in the unwinnable, unending race to have more. But most of us in the middle, sensing something rotten about YOYO society, shield our children from its excesses. One parent, for example, worried about the unbridled competitiveness and con-sumerism to which her impressionable teenaged daughter was daily exposed to, confessed her misgivings: "You just hope your child doesn't have anorexia of the soul."[19] Plenty of parents undoubtedly harbor similar worries, feel guilty, or second-guess themselves for failing to master our culture's exhausting juggling act.

Let's stop second-guessing ourselves and start leading humanity along a new path. This misguided "civilization of self" is not work-ing for any of us, whether we are wealthy, impoverished, or some-where in between. Each of us can face that fact, toss away this misguided strategy for living, liberate ourselves from the culture's confusion of means and ends, and lead ourselves and our families in a new direction.

Granted, we cannot control the course of geopolitical crises or even have any say in whether our own employer will cut jobs next week; we cannot eliminate the radical uncertainties about the future that so characterize modern life and work. But we will attain greater peace, fulfillment, and empowerment as soon as we start reclaiming control where we can, starting with our own sense of what makes life meaningful. We can stop living outside in—that is, futilely chasing validation or satisfaction based on what we own, how we look, or what others think of us. We can start living inside out—looking within ourselves to find meaning and purpose. Instead of bowing to cultural icons who proclaim that happiness is about self-aggrandizement, we can proclaim that meaning and fulfillment ultimately arise from looking out for the whole human community and not only for ourselves.

An American tragedy illustrates the point. Recall Hurricane Katrina in 2005, which wrecked New Orleans and bereaved the most impoverished citizens of the earth's most prosperous country. While most Americans marveled at their government's apparent indifference to its poorest, some New Orleanians marveled about something else: the outpouring of solidarity that galvanized many communities. Those who had lost much helped those who had lost even more; those who might have stewed bitterly over the devastation they suffered instead found positive energy by helping their neighbors rebuild. One observer drew this conclusion after watching his neighbors in action: "When you think about it, if your main goal is to be happy, you're going to be miserable; but if your main goal is to love, you're going to be happy."[20]

That bold, counterintuitive observation suggests a very different kind of strategy: if we want to find fulfillment, we ought to pursue it not by serving only ourselves but by taking more care of those around us. Good strategists first understand where they are and then decide where they want to go. We've chronicled the current civilization of self and its discontents. Let's leave behind the civilization that gave us Garbage Kingdom and lead ourselves, and our neighbors, toward a different sort of civilization, a new kind of kingdom.

How do you interpret the world you've inherited? In what ways are we heading in the right direction? In what ways are we heading off track?

Small though your role may seem, how have you been shaping our culture and leading our world, for good and for ill?

What kind of civilization have you been creating by how you treat others, spend money, raise children, or engage in your work?

Discover Your Mighty Purpose

Evaluate the world you've inherited.
» Envision the future worth fighting for.
Articulate a purpose worth living for.
Embrace values worth standing for.
Put heart into strategy to give it life.

4
—

Where Will You Lead Us?
Envision the Future Worth Fighting For

I have a dream that my four children will one day live in a nation where they will not be judged by the color of their skin but by the content of their character . . . [that] little black boys and black girls will be able to join hands with little white boys and white girls and walk together as sisters and brothers."[1]

The previous chapter developed snapshots of the present, including the harsh reality that children are swarming garbage dumps in Manila. This chapter invites us to picture the future, a future we will be willing to fight for, just as Dr. King fought for—but never lived to see—the day when black and white children would "walk together as sisters and brothers."

Why spend the time trying to envision an idealistic future that we might not live long enough to experience? The first-century Roman philosopher Seneca put it this way: "If one does not know to which port one is sailing, no wind is favorable."[2] Many centuries later, the Harvard Business School professor John Kotter described a good leader's first task as "establishing direction: developing a vision of the future—often the distant future."[3] The word *vision* connotes something seen, and visionaries peer past their own lifetimes to see a future worth the investment of their time, talent, and energy.

We need such visionaries—not cynics, idle dreamers, or slick spin doctors, but everyday visionaries committed to turning a desirable future into reality, for our own children and for all children. Rather than hunker down with the 60 percent of Americans who despair that their children will have a worse life than they have, can we be visionary enough to struggle for something better that will outlive us, a world that will be better for all children in generations to come?

Every human and spiritual tradition worth our allegiance is visionary in its aspirations for humanity. Dr. King's dream, for example, drew from the U.S. Declaration of Independence, which proclaims the self-evident truth that all of us are created equal; more profoundly, Dr. King hearkened to the assurance in the book of Genesis that all humans are created in God's image and likeness.

And so it has been for visionaries throughout human history. The medieval Jewish thinker Maimonides envisioned a time of "no famine, no war, no envy, no strife."[4] He was drawing from the prophet Isaiah's vision that, one day, "the wolf shall live with the lamb, the leopard shall lie down with the kid . . . and the weaned child shall put his hand on the adder's den. They will not hurt or destroy on all my holy mountain" (Isaiah 11:6, 8–9).

Such words may sound comforting, but in fact they should discomfit us. We should hear them not as poetic abstraction but as a call to action. They are a vision, not a mirage, and the difference between vision and mirage often lies in our willingness to act.

We can begin by reflecting on a vision drawn from my own spiritual tradition. I imagine how quickly (and positively) this world would change if 2 billion of us Christians struggled on behalf of that vision and were joined in the fight by the billions more who also aspire to a more just, peaceful, and loving civilization.

A Vision Transcending All Boundaries

A common refrain echoes with increasing momentum as the globe spins from Saturday's darkness into Sunday's dawn: "Our Father, who art in heaven . . ." The multilingual fugue begins in sparsely populated Pacific atolls before crescendoing in the densely Christian Philippines. A few hours later, Our Fathers are proclaimed in Africa's exuberant, growing churches and murmured in Europe's elegant but ever emptier churches before finding fuller voice across the Atlantic in the countries boasting Christendom's largest populations: the United States, Brazil, and Mexico.

Brazil's evangelicals pray more exuberantly than staid U.S. Quakers and Episcopalians. But North Americans are a no-less-pious breed for their subdued style: witness the intricate choreography of Catholic church parking lots emptied and refilled multiple times each Sunday to accommodate throngs of Christians at services too tightly timed to permit either impromptu Spirit-led outbursts or long-winded sermons (well, rarely the former, but occasionally the latter).

I've prayed the Our Father in more countries than I can easily count, often standing beside Christians whose words I couldn't fathom. Although the words often eluded me, comprehension rarely did. The Our Father flows by a common cadence in most languages, and even when temporarily thrown off the trail by foreign words, I usually rejoined my brothers and sisters at the pauses that punctuated each sentence, ". . . on earth, as it is in heaven." And though common language was frequently missing, solidarity never was. I've felt welcomed to pray the Our Father alongside Tamils, Japanese, and Kenyans, and equally alongside Methodists, Lutherans, and Presbyterians.

"Our Father . . . thy kingdom come." Few phrases are uttered so widely or so regularly. Democrats pray it, as do Republicans; so do Red Sox fans and Yankees fans, Catholics and Pentecostals.

Rwandan Hutus prayed for the kingdom to come, as did the Tutsi neighbors they later butchered so savagely. Belfast's Protestants and Catholics prayed for the kingdom to come as too many bloody Sundays dawned in their decades-long feud. The engineers of South African apartheid prayed for the kingdom, as did black South Africans who wouldn't dare sit beside them in church. Many millions of us will pray for the kingdom to come today before sitting down to abundant meals in comfortable dwellings, while millions of others will pray for the kingdom but eat no full meal this day.

What are we Christians to make of ourselves? We claim a common Father, yet we don't always treat our brothers and sisters accordingly. The first letter of John pronounces blunt judgment: "Those who say, 'I love God,' and hate their brothers or sisters, are liars; for those who do not love a brother or sister whom they have seen, cannot love God whom they have not seen" (1 John 4:20). We aren't seeing clearly, John tells us; we lack vision. Faulty vision similarly afflicts those of us who have stood by passively while our brothers and sisters starve, become refugees, remain mired in poverty, or suffer countless other privations. Pope Benedict XVI put it plainly: "closing our eyes to our neighbor also blinds us to God." [5]

We have lost sight of the vision that our shared prayer proclaims—"thy kingdom come." Do we even know what our vision is, or what it truly entails? Jesus sometimes spoke of it cryptically (who can blame him?—he had neither PowerPoint slides nor media coaches to sharpen his presentation). Some of us associate this kingdom with the afterlife or the end of time, so mostly we wait around for it. One of my acquaintances looks forward to eternal respite from "getting up for work, no subways, no income tax—total peace and serenity." That sounds like a great vision to me!

But Jesus proclaimed that a kingdom "has come near" and "is among you" (Mark 1:15; Luke 17:21). It erupted into human history in an entirely new way when he did, and it will come to fullness, as one friend puts it, when we recognize "that God is in every piece of creation, and that all creation, without exception, is sacred." Or as another friend said: "We know the kingdom has come when God's will is done—when love of God above all else, and when love of neighbors as oneself, determine our thoughts, words, and deeds."

Jesus would agree. When his often-confused inner circle argued about who was "greatest in the kingdom," Jesus explained his vision by pointing to a child: "whoever becomes humble like this child is the greatest in the kingdom of heaven. Whoever welcomes one such child in my name welcomes me" (Matthew 18:1, 4–5). Another Gospel account of the same incident elaborates further: "Whoever wants to be first must be last of all and servant of all" (Mark 9:35). In other words, the kingdom is a child welcomed and cared for, a world in which those who have power, influence, resources, and authority struggle to make life better for those who don't.

Jesus then offers a contrast. "If any of you put a stumbling block before one of these little ones who believe in me, it would better for you if a great millstone were fastened around your neck and you were drowned in the depth of the sea" (Matthew 18:6). The opposite of the kingdom is a place in which children are caused "to stumble," where those who have resources and influence mistreat those who don't.

The sad reality is that our children are stumbling, all over God's creation. It is estimated that 640 million children lack adequate shelter around the world; 140 million children have never been to school; 90 million children are starving. Fifteen million children have lost parents to AIDS.[6] Older translations of Proverbs 29:18 proclaim, "Without vision, the people perish," and our children are perishing because too few of us get the vision that 2 billion of us proclaim.

Fortunately, many millions of everyday visionaries do get it. They fortify our children against stumbling and lift them up whenever they fall.

What expressions of vision do you find within your faith tradition, from your family, at work, or from other sources that have shaped your worldview?

Are any of those visionary words "alive" to you, and, if so, how do they influence the way you live?

Treated Like Part of the Royal Family

My first taste of Royal Family Kids' Camps (RFKC) was not as strong as I had anticipated. As attendees sat down to the celebratory banquet preceding their annual conference, I noted the floral centerpiece, fine cutlery, and—hmm, no wine glasses. No alcohol. That's not what we Irish Catholics from New York City have in mind when we're invited to a celebration.

Still, if these devout Christians, many representing evangelical denominations, understand the word *celebrate* differently from us ethnic Catholics of the urban Northeast, we all nonetheless understand what *Our Father* means and what that Father's kingdom ought to mean for kids.

If it's our Father's kingdom, then all of us, even the kids no one wants, are part of a royal family, no? That logic has been driving Wayne Tesch since 1985, when he scraped together a few hundred dollars to start a small, one-week camp to serve children in the foster-care system. That was 150 camps, 6,000 volunteers, and thousands of neglected children ago. Since that first camp, Wayne has barnstormed the country, happily visiting any church of any denomination that's willing to learn about—and perhaps share—his vision of the kingdom. Lots of church communities have done so, agreeing to sponsor an annual summer camp for children in foster care. After requisite training, adult volunteers in their forties, fifties, and sixties find themselves doing jobs they thought they'd left behind with their teenage years: serving as camp counselors in non-air-conditioned cabins, swatting at mosquitoes, and leading preteen kids through hikes, swim classes, and arts-and-crafts projects.

Glenda Jay of Pottsville, Arkansas, who has nearly two decades of professional experience as a quality engineer, could probably find plenty of reengineering projects in the rustic—make that all-but-primitive—camp where she and colleagues tend a few dozen young children each summer. Unfortunately, what she would most like to reengineer is the only thing she can't: the upbringing of her young campers. Plenty of them have been through two failed adoptions by their tenth birthday. Some of them have known the indignity of "dragging their things to the street in suitcases and garbage bags so the social worker could drive them to the next home."[7] These are kids who don't visit relatives on holidays because they don't know their relatives, and their relatives aren't searching them out either. As Glenda puts it, they are kids "that others have given up on."

Of course, in some cases these kids are better off without their relatives. Californian Melinda Hahn, another volunteer camp counselor, would undoubtedly like to reengineer the father of a seven-year-old I'll call Felicia; before Felicia found her way into the foster-care system, Dad's idea of parenting was to tie Felicia to a chair to keep her still during a movie.

How do you make a positive impact on a kid who has been through that? Glenda tries to do so by "being a loving, compassionate adult who is there to serve them and not to hurt them." Melinda echoes the theme when recalling the shy, overweight, pigeon-toed seven-year-old I'll call Jane, who traipsed through redwood trees baffled both by the forest's majesty and by her first exposure to a place different from her hometown streets. As Melinda put it, "I tried to treat Jane like royalty and told her how beautiful she was, that she was God's creation"—as marvelous in her own way as a redwood, despite her pigeon-toed, overweight self-consciousness.

Nearly 3 million cases of child neglect, abuse, or abandonment are reported in the United States each year. The RFKC camps cater to a few thousand. Doesn't it discourage Wayne and his colleagues to think that their work amounts to little more than a few drops in the bucket? He answers with some aquatic imagery of his own. He tells the story of a man walking the beach who meets a young child who is retrieving starfish stranded by the receding tide and gently placing them back in the water. "Hey kid," the man says, "look around. There must be a thousand starfish stranded on this beach. You think you're going to save them all?" "No," replies the kid, picking up another starfish, "but I'm going to save this one."[8]

Cynical New Yorkers like me tend to roll our eyes at that kind of story. We'll point out the great burden carried by abused children and their uncertain and excruciating journey to whole, happy adulthood. Yes, RFKC's committed volunteers might manage to save a few starfish during that precious week they have with these children, but for many others, that week might have little lasting impact.

Glenda, Melinda, and all their colleagues know that, of course. Their vision isn't a fantasy. Rather, faith in their vision is what steels them through the seemingly impossible challenges of turning it into reality. They embody the spirit that the management researcher Peter Senge describes in *The Fifth Discipline*: "Truly creative people use the gap between vision and current reality to generate energy for change."[9]

Often enough, energy for change means the willingness to fight. "Hope is something that was taken from these kids at a very early age, and without hope, there may not be a reason to 'fight,'" says Glenda. "I want to give these kids something to fight for, if only, for the moment, that means the chance to come back to camp again next year."

So Glenda keeps fighting for the kids and sparking a few of them to fight for themselves. She fights to show them "what it means to be part of a 'royal family' and part of the 'kingdom of God.'" The kingdom is no sterile abstraction but something to fight for.

A hemisphere away, someone else is fighting on the kingdom's behalf.

Walking up the Hill and down the Hill

Sr. Saturnina Devia first traveled from her native Spain to Venezuela in 1956 on a weeks-long odyssey by car, train, bus, and ship. She must have felt as if she were journeying to the end of the world, and in a sense, she was. After arriving in Caracas, Sr. Saturnina and two colleagues kept going, first by bus to where the buses stopped at the end of the paved roads, and from there by foot. Caracas sits at the base of a bowl rimmed by lush hills that eventually link into the high-peaked Andes. The hills are beautiful to behold but torturous to climb; imagine doing so, as Sr. Saturnina and her colleagues did—in 1950s-edition nun's habits on steamy summer days in this city not far from the equator.

Nonetheless, walk they did—up the hill and down the hill, one hour of walking each way, two hours of walking each day. In those days, there were no schools in the hilly outskirts of Caracas known as Petare, nor for that matter were there roads, running water, or much else that we associate with civilization.

But there were children of poor Venezuelans, and Sr. Saturnina herded some 250 of these children into a three-sided shed with a tin roof. She taught them to read and write, stopping each day when about an hour of daylight still remained so that she and her colleagues could safely make their way back down through the rutted fields. Each morning the cycle began anew: up the hill and down the hill, creating the kingdom a few students at a time.

Much has changed since Sr. Saturnina's arrival. The sisters eventually built a little convent among those they served. Nowadays their pupils, some of Latin America's poorest children, study not in an open shack but in clean, well-appointed classrooms. Each student now enjoys a daily hot meal at school, and those with colds or fevers visit the small clinic that Sr. Saturnina oversees. Paved (if potholed) roads now snake through Petare, so neither Sr. Saturnina nor visitors to her school have to clamber uphill by foot.

Still, Sr. Saturnina must have complicated feelings whenever she travels these roads. No longer do rutted fields snag anyone's ankles, because virtually no open spaces remain on the expansive hillside. Instead, ramshackle dwellings perch precariously one atop another as Caracas's growing population of the impoverished cram into every spare nook of this slum. Each newly completed roof of scavenged scrap becomes the foundation for an even more ramshackle dwelling that soon totters atop it. It's hard to believe that these stacked houses of little more than cards remain standing. And sometimes they don't. When heavy rains fall, so occasionally do some of the houses in a landslide that temporarily (if brutally) culls Petare's population of poor before new arrivals take their place.

Sr. Saturnina and her colleagues are teaching far more children than they did in 1956, but they don't keep pace with the population growth of Petare. And the school began serving meals to pupils mainly because it had to; children who couldn't count on getting a decent meal at home were sometimes fainting in class—not very conducive to learning. And the school offers these children love and bright classrooms because some will return home to windowless shacks where a single parent, overwhelmed by poverty's challenges or beset by substance-abuse problems, can't or won't provide the love every child deserves.

Sr. Saturnina left her family and native land to invest five decades of her life in this place, and in some ways, Petare has been sliding downhill ever since she started walking uphill. I wondered what she makes of it all and how this devout woman connects Petare's apparently godforsaken present reality with the promise of the kingdom.

"The kingdom of God," she replies, "*se hace presente*—it's coming alive, it's making itself present, it's here." It's making itself present most visibly whenever she provides the love, education, and support that will enable people "to live with the dignity that corresponds to children of God's kingdom." For this woman, the kingdom is not what Marx derided as the "opiate of the masses," a dreamy distraction from an unjust present. Rather, this kingdom is "what I've been working for from my very first day here until today." Then, perhaps picturing the children she serves, she rephrases her mission, using words one doesn't expect to hear from a kindly senior citizen in matronly eyeglasses and a nun's habit: "This kingdom is what I've been working for . . . No, it's something that I've been fighting for, struggling for."

Envisioning a New Civilization

Wayne Tesch of RFKC once reflected on the indignities suffered by the neglected children he's privileged to serve, "Sometimes it seems as if all the evil we adults manage to perpetrate eventually spirals down to the doorstep of some little kid."

He's right. Children suffer when we in the adult world saddle them with our problems and misjudgments. They bear the brunt of our wars, negligence, self-centeredness, or irresponsibility. How disgraceful that we adults, generation after generation, afflict little children with the consequences of our poor choices. As Jesus might put it when describing the antithesis of his kingdom, these little children are stumbling because we've caused them to stumble.

Children don't decide to grow up impoverished, malnourished, and illiterate, amid violence or without medical care. Children start no wars, allocate no national budgets, and make no health-care policies. And when white girls and black boys don't walk hand in hand, it's only because we in the adult world have taught them not to.

How terribly discouraging it must be for Wayne Tesch, Sr. Saturnina, and so many teachers, doctors, counselors, loving parents, coaches, and others to feel as if they are futilely trying to hold back a relentless tide.

Yet most everyday visionaries never seem to feel discouraged for very long, perhaps because for every adult who causes a child to stumble there are countless others who are catching them when they fall, bringing them up in loving homes, teaching them to read, and making the world safe for them. These legions vindicate Jesus' claim that his kingdom "is like a mustard seed, which, when sown upon the ground, is the smallest of all the seeds on earth; yet when it is sown it grows up and becomes the greatest of all shrubs" (Mark 4:31–32).

From tiny seeds great things grow. Sr. Saturnina, one of a lonely few in 1956, now counts herself among nearly forty thousand people across sixteen Latin American countries who teach 1 million impoverished students each year in the network that is fittingly called Fe y Alegría, or "Faith and Joy." This is how the organization's founder explained the name. "We are messengers of the Faith and at the same time messengers of Joy. . . . They are two powers and two gifts of God which can transform the world." [10]

They are messengers of faith "which can transform the world." How true. Too often, what passes for vision in pop culture or among politicians is hollow sloganeering or focus-group-tested jargon. But true visionaries are true believers. They have the courage of their convictions because they have convictions. They transform others only because they themselves have been transformed by the power and majesty of their beliefs. And steeled by their beliefs, they can willingly persevere in seemingly impossible quests to repair the world.

Also, they are messengers of joy, which can transform the world. How true, and how sad, that *joyful* is a word we seldom hear anymore. And how ironic that whereas a previous chapter reported so many apparently joyless, prosperous people in the United States, these companions of Latin America's poorest describe themselves as messengers of joy. And how remarkable that they can be joyful, these David-sized men and women who are slinging rocks at the Goliath-sized challenges of poverty and neglect.

They are joyful because through their vision they have transcended themselves: they work for something bigger than themselves, their egos, and their lifetimes. The American naturalist Henry David Thoreau put it this way: "If a man constantly aspires, is he not elevated." [11] They are elevated by the beauty and nobility of their aspirations for humanity. Paradoxically, every time Sr. Saturnina or Wayne Tesch or their many colleagues reach out to lift up a downtrodden neighbor, they themselves are lifted up in the process.

Finally, they are joyful—and peaceful—because they understand that they are not building their own kingdom, but God's, to be fulfilled in God's good time and in God's ways, not ours. Archbishop

Óscar Romero, gunned down by paramilitaries who were irritated by his kingdom-building advocacy on behalf of El Salvador's peasants, once said, "We cannot do everything, and there is a sense of liberation in realizing that. This enables us to do something and do it very well. It may be incomplete, but it is a beginning, a step along the way and an opportunity for God's grace to enter and do the rest." Mother Teresa, who spent much of her life tending to the inexhaustible supply of the destitute and dying on Calcutta's streets, spoke similarly: "We cannot do great things on this earth. We can only do little things with great love."

And so they struggle, as Sr. Saturnina puts it. But, like her, they struggle joyfully as they daily walk up the hills and down the hills that are life's great challenges. They joyfully save one starfish at a time. They know that the kingdom is here, *se hace presente*—it's alive, making itself present, and is among us in every heart that welcomes and loves a child, or teaches one, or protects one from danger.

The promise of this kingdom—a place of peace, justice, righteousness, and joy—is a promise for everyone, of course, not solely for children. But children uniquely embody our hopes for the future. They inherit whatever world we've shaped, and they will lead civilization forward when we've passed on. So it's no wonder that visionaries like Jesus or Dr. King so often used the image of a child to inspire our visions of a worthy future.

Jesus the visionary once proclaimed his kingdom "not of this world," and for Christians, its theological significance transcends our earthly lives. But its defining characteristics and values—justice, peace, and love—call Christians to transform this world, even as they await another. And billions more of us, representing other great spiritual traditions, champion these same values. All of us can join the common cause and fight for a more just, peaceful, and loving world. By struggling to transform our world, we can find the satisfaction that the nineteenth-century British writer George Bernard Shaw described: "This is the true joy of life, the being used for a purpose recognized by yourself as a mighty one." [12]

Granted, few of us will walk the hills of South American slums or guide orphan campers on nature walks, but all of us can nonetheless walk together. For we bankers, lawyers, parents, and teachers are, for good or for ill, shaping civilization, the total culture of our era, as the dictionary defines that word. As we negotiate deals, manage our households, vote for presidents, spend our surplus savings, and carry out myriad other daily acts, we are leading our world to justice and peace—or we are not. A leader's first task, as pointed out at this chapter's opening, is to develop "a vision of the future—often the distant future." Let's turn ourselves into leaders, people who have thought deeply about the future and who care deeply enough about it to struggle alongside Sr. Saturnina for the mighty purpose of creating a new kind of planet, a new kind of civilization, distinguished, as a late pope once said, by the "magnificence of human virtue, people's goodness, collective prosperity, and true civilization: the civilization of love."[13]

How would a civilization of love, characterized by the "magnificence of human virtue, people's goodness, collective prosperity" look different from our present reality?

What living people do you consider visionary, and why?

What is your vision—that is, what future are you willing to labor for?

Discover Your Mighty Purpose

Evaluate the world you've inherited.
Envision the future worth fighting for.
» Articulate a purpose worth living for.
Embrace values worth standing for.
Put heart into strategy to give it life.

5
—

Why Are You Here?
Articulate a Purpose Worth Living For

A ndrew Muras felt pulled in different directions: "For years I had wondered if my role in the world was to try and do great things at work, or have a good family, or be a good father, provider, and husband. What was I here for, and how did I make a difference?"

Why am I here? When we can't answer that daunting question, we drift through life, which becomes a succession of loosely linked episodes. We are here on earth to get a good job after school, then to earn enough to buy a house, then to ward off boredom at work and the anxiety that we aren't earning enough for a comfortable retirement. On reaching retirement, we wonder what to do with the rest of our lives. In the worst case, we might look back over a busy lifetime, wonder what gave it purpose, and conclude with the gloomy Macbeth that life was "a tale / Told by an idiot, full of sound and fury, / Signifying nothing."[1]

Why am I here? When we ponder the question and answer it well, life becomes a meaningful tale that signifies much. We conceive some unifying purpose that ties together life's discrete activities, connects our deepest beliefs to what we do all week, and restores meaning to work. We articulate some role on earth that transforms us from dreamers to visionaries. That is, we don't merely wish for a better world, a civilization of love, or the kingdom; we feel called to help turn that vision into reality. We aspire to nothing less than to transform the world but are humble enough to start by transforming our own hearts, and we do that by committing to a worthy purpose.

Let's start by visiting two people who have found their purpose. Although their backgrounds, lifestyles, and professions could hardly be more different, both are leading our civilization in a common direction, and they implicitly invite us to join them.

His Purpose Is to Be Holy

Most conscientious working parents can identify with the struggles Andrew Muras articulates in this chapter's opening: the competing demands of work, family, religion, and community pull them to pieces. Parents shuttle children to schools and practices, shuttle themselves on out-of-town business trips, and volunteer some remaining sliver of free time for church or community events. They're doing lots of things, they sometimes feel they are doing none of them particularly well, and they occasionally lose track of themselves in the process.

Countless marriages collapse as partners start pulling apart when they need to pull closer together. Andrew is proud of a marriage that has entered its second happy decade, quite an achievement considering that his jealous mistress demanded hours of daily attention, frequent out-of-town trips, and near 24/7 cell-phone availability. That mistress? His job at a leading, multinational aerospace company. Although much was asked of him, he has been thrilled to work for a great company in a highly technical, fast-moving industry that challenged his talents while rewarding him well.

Andrew realized, though, that his juggling act would no longer work when yet another suitor arrived to clamor for attention and affection: his first child, a baby girl. After some anguished deliberation, prayer, and number crunching, Andrew did what few dare to do: he downshifted from the corporate passing lane by cutting back to the equivalent of a four-day workweek. Credit him with courage; plenty of us have contemplated similar lifestyle changes at the peak of our earnings and career trajectory, only to balk, "Not me, and not yet."

But although Andrew's tough choice to trade income for family time brought greater balance to his life and better reflected his priorities, it was merely a better, more manageable version of the same split life he had been living. He was still juggling, and over time his religious beliefs started to feel like another ball in this circus act, another task to be wedged into a crowded schedule. He half considered focusing on his demanding career while young and deferring piety until later: "I thought that maybe I needed to wait until retirement for real spiritual development." But he quickly dismissed this half-baked concept of sequencing career and spirituality, as if the latter were a hobby one takes up when life's "real" work is done. "That can't be what God wants," he says.

He looked for other solutions. Some Christians, for example, sport bracelets with the letters WWJD as a reminder to ask themselves when mulling over major decisions, "What would Jesus do?" But that technique, which works for many people, didn't work for Andrew. "The problem is, I really don't know what Jesus would do. He never dealt with sales quotas and company policies, or choosing a benefits option and a 401(k) plan."

So, What Would Andrew Do to integrate his work, family, and spirituality? His breakthrough was the realization that the path to greater wholeness and happiness lay not in rescheduling life but in fundamentally rethinking how spirituality, life, and work fit together. He found the solution in a sense of purpose that ties together his life, even when it feels as if daily life's unending demands are pulling him in multiple directions. What was his solution? Be holy.

Be holy? That sounds like a life's purpose for monks in monasteries, not for corporate vice presidents in the aerospace industry. I'm stressed over hitting this month's sales target; my daughter has taken ill and needs to be picked up at school; my retirement savings are shrinking in a stock-market decline; and you're telling me to be holy?

Precisely, and if we unravel what holiness means, we'll understand why it works for Andrew. Andrew's symptom is ours as well: a life disintegrating because it's pulled in so many directions. We need to integrate ourselves again by finding some meaning or purpose that will make us feel whole. In fact, that is exactly what *integrate* means: the word's Latin root means "whole."

But what exactly does holiness have to do with wholeness? Our medieval ancestors intuited the connection centuries ago; the Old English root of the word *holy* means "whole" or "happy." Holy people are whole people because they manage to integrate their lives around some unifying purpose. That purpose is not a new job or career, but a new way of thinking and living. More specifically, the holy have ordered their lives around the spiritual beliefs and values they consider ultimately important. Their wholeness manifests itself in a consistent approach to everything and everyone: their actions correspond with their words, they treat subordinates the same way as they treat their bosses, and they model an unvaried set of virtues—even when no one is watching. For these reasons, we say they have *integrity*, yet another related word.

Rabbi Lawrence Kushner helps us further understand the connection between holiness and whole lives. He defines holiness as "being aware that you are in the presence of God."[2] Most of us are aware of God's presence when we gather at mosque, church, or temple. Then we go home and God (in a sense) disappears. We relapse into de-energizing, split-life thinking in which work is work, religion is religion, and rarely do the two collide. But the rabbi is saying something quite different: holiness is awareness of God's presence always. God is present after we've left church or temple: in that meeting to discuss sales quotas, in the ethical dilemma with which our team is wrestling, or in the wonder of an intellectually rigorous analysis excellently presented. God is even present in the humanity of that annoying colleague who talks too much at the meeting.

The prophet Isaiah proclaims, "Holy, holy, holy is the Lord . . . the whole earth is full of his glory" (Isaiah 6:3). The *whole* earth is full, the prophet tells us, not just the churches, or the inspiring sunsets, or the people I like, or the religion I myself practice. God is a unifying presence throughout every moment and aspect of my harried life, and my becoming aware of God's presence is the thread that can tie each day's disparate activities into one whole life. The rabbi draws out the implication of trying to live this way: "What more appropriate overarching principle could there be than for God to tell us that we ourselves must act in such a way so as to remind one another of the presence of God."[3]

Ignatius of Loyola agreed with the way Rabbi Kushner looks at the world, for Ignatius instructed Jesuits to "find God in all things." And one of his spiritual sons, the Jesuit paleontologist and mystic Pierre Teilhard de Chardin, distills from that phrase a pathway to filling our every action with meaning and awe. "God . . . is not remote from us," Fr. de Chardin wrote. "On the contrary, at every moment he awaits us in the activity, the work to be done. . . . He is, in a sense, at the point of my pen, my pick, my paint-brush, my needle—and my heart and my thought."[4]

God awaits us in the intellectually challenging problem at work, in the opportunity to support a colleague rather than stab him in the back, in every negotiation we undertake, in our reaction to disappointment, in the woman who needs a seat during our train commute home, in the spouse we kiss upon arriving, in the dirty diapers we change, and in the homework help we give before flopping into bed exhausted. Before, Andrew had been trying to fit together tasks and obligations that didn't seem to have much to do with one another; now, these all become dimensions of one greater task: being holy by finding God's presence in everything he does.

Work, then, does not distract or divert him from his life's purpose; it is fundamentally part of his journey to greater holiness, a way for him to develop his God-given talents, transform the world into a better place, and find God present in colleagues and clients. Andrew says, "I can't separate my work life—where I spend the majority of my waking hours—from my spiritual growth. Instead, work—and what I do there—is continuing to [be] an essential element of who I am as a person and who I am becoming over time."

As a Christian, Andrew naturally looks to Jesus as a model of holiness at work. After all, according to tradition, Jesus devoted far more years to carpentry than to publicly preaching God's kingdom, and we can presume that his time working in a "normal" job was not time wasted. As Andrew sees it, all of Jesus' work, whether as craftsman, healer, or teacher, ultimately had "a focus on others rather than on the self, a focus on abandoning self-centeredness and attachments and instead being concerned for and about others." To be holy, as Andrew has come to see it, is to be "for" others, at home and at work and in his community.

Holy Organizations Work Better

It turns out that Andrew's aim to be a holy professional might also make him a more effective professional. That counterintuitive, even startling, conclusion emerges from research done by the Harvard Business School management professors John Kotter and James Heskett. Certainly, the very last thing these professors thought they were researching was holiness in the workplace! The *h* word, as best I can tell, crops up nowhere in their literature. But they have plenty to say about the value of being for others.

In *Corporate Culture and Performance*, the academics explored the cultural characteristics that distinguish the best-performing companies from the weaker ones. Managers at great companies concentrate on serving clients well, consider how to make team members more effective and productive, and strive to deliver outstanding financial returns for their shareholder owners. In other words, these high-performing managers go through their days mindful of others—customers, subordinates, and shareholders. As Andrew would put it, they are consciously being for others.

In contrast, the research showed that managers at lousy companies mostly worry about themselves. They scheme to get ahead of the pack at the expense of peers, use their subordinates to make themselves look good, and take advantage of customers and shareholders to stuff a few more pennies into their own pockets. The Harvard researchers summarized their findings this way: "If the managers at the lower-performing firms do not value highly their customers, their stockholders, or their employees, what do they care about? When asked, our interviewees most often said: 'Themselves.'"[5]

More recently, researcher Jim Collins has echoed those themes in the best-selling *Good to Great*, in which he speaks of "Level Five" leaders as the pinnacle role models of high-quality organizational leadership because they "are ambitious first and foremost for the cause, the organization, the work—not themselves."[6]

But the real challenge, which neither Collins nor other management theorists address, is how to turn ourselves into people who care more about the cause than about ourselves. It's especially difficult to instill that attitude in private-sector companies, where greed and personal ambition can run so rampant that the whole organization runs not in pursuit of a great cause beyond self but of maximizing pay, power, and status for self.

Let's be frank: companies can't instill a sense of purpose beyond self; it's an attitude that people either bring to work or don't. And most of those who bring that attitude to work ground it, as Andrew does, in their deepest beliefs about how people ought to live, work, and treat one another. So the clear, if ironic, implication of the management research just cited is that our worldly enterprises will perform best by attracting leaders who manifest a deeply spiritual sense of purpose beyond themselves.

We began with Andrew Muras's split-life quandary: "For years I had wondered if my role in the world was to try and do great things at work, or have a good family, or be a good father, provider, and husband. What was I here for, and how did I make a difference?" His question ultimately revolved around his purpose in life, and his answer—"I am here on earth to be holy"—has pulled his life together and filled its every gesture with potential meaning, whether at home or at work.

In what ways does your life feel split and in what ways whole?

If one definition of holiness is "awareness of God's presence," can you bring to mind three moments of God being present in yesterday's work, problems, thoughts, or conversations?

Her Purpose Is to Repair the World

Commerce rarely pauses on 138th Street in New York's South Bronx. Street vendors hustle for business, shoppers hunt down bargains, the occasional panhandler begs for loose change, and drivers jockey for too-few parking spots as the whole neighborhood rushes to the merengue beat that pulses from storefront to storefront.

Shoppers lug bags laden with bargain purchases from $.99 stores; mothers push infants in baby carriages; harried delivery people balance pizzas while weaving through crowds; and soft-spoken Nanette Schorr wheels along a rolling airline carry-on crammed with court documents and complicated case files. You and I might flip through those pages and find only abstruse legal language that adds up to a monumental headache, but Nanette finds stories of human struggle that add up to a purpose worth living for. She represents impoverished parents who have been separated from their children by court order. An observer might say she spends her time doing legal work; but as she sees it, she spends her days "helping parents and children find the opportunity to most fully express their love and care for one another."

Most of us feel lucky if our work enables us to develop and express our talents and interests. People like Nanette and Andrew Muras are luckier still. Their work also helps express an answer to a crucial question, What is my purpose in the world?

Psychologists say that most of us don't typically start asking that question until well into adulthood. Recall that Andrew Muras only asked and answered those questions after competing work and family demands forced him to.

In Nanette's case, the seeds of purpose were sowed in childhood by parents who stressed that we are here on earth not to insulate ourselves from the world's sorrows and imperfections, but to right its injustices. Her rabbi father saw a commitment to justice as fundamental to Jewish faith; the book of Leviticus, for example, commands us to "not render an unjust judgment . . . with justice you shall judge your neighbor" (19:15).

That abstract ideal—creating a more just world—found concrete expression in the civil-rights campaigners, women's movement activists, and other social activists that Nanette studied or worked alongside during her student years. Nanette eventually found her own way to struggle for justice. As a lawyer and director at Legal Services of New York, she represents domestic-violence victims, poor tenants facing eviction orders, or parents whose children have been removed from their care by government agencies.

Nanette's work embodies a simple yet profound ideal drawn from her spiritual tradition, that we humans are here for *tikkun olam* (in Hebrew)—that is, "to repair the world," or "perfect" a world that has wandered far from that perfect order that reigned on the seventh biblical day when God's creative work was finished.

Tikkun would have echoed constantly in Nanette's young life, as part of the Aleinu prayer that culminates most Jewish congregational services. In Nanette's case, prayer has evolved into purpose, as she repairs the world in places that most need it.

Jesuit theologian Fr. Jim Keenan speaks of mercy as "the willingness to enter the chaos of others to answer them in their need."[7] If that's true, Nanette is among our most merciful, for she's chosen to enter the most chaotic of lives. Plainly put, she works with people whom society often shuns. Some clients have not only lost custody of their children but, she says, also are "in debt, unemployed, and facing multiple, conflicting irresolvable demands on their time." Some blundered into bad relationships with substance abusers who brought more grief than support to their young children. Others, blindsided by serious illness or lost jobs, spiraled steadily downward as late rent payments and unfilled medical prescriptions led to eviction notices and worsening health. Still others are teenage mothers who are facing adult responsibilities without high school diplomas, jobs, or parenting skills.

Whatever their circumstances, people arrive in Nanette's office feeling alone, isolated, and worthless—"stigmatized," as she puts it, "as someone who has neglected or been unable to care properly for their own children." So her first task is not building a case file, but rebuilding her client's sense of dignity. To do so she draws not on the case citations that cram her lawyer's head, but on a verse recalled from the first-century Rabbi Hillel: "Pass not judgment upon thy neighbor until thou has put oneself in his place." When she does so, Nanette can come to "admire and respect their great fortitude, persistence and compassion in dealing with unbelievably difficult situations."

They need whatever fortitude they can muster. For understandable reasons, no conscientious judge or city bureaucrat risks releasing a child into a family environment that could prove harmful, even in cases where children have been removed from a parent because of bad information or misunderstanding. Cases often drag on for a year or more of court visits, petitions, negotiations with city agencies, and client enrollment in substance-abuse programs or parenting skills classes. Nanette needs persistence and fortitude, too, for while she is painstakingly helping her clients, they may be hurting themselves: "We work so hard, and our clients disappoint us. They miss appointments, they miss court dates, they express anger in all the wrong places, including sometimes at us; they mistrust us." As a result, she admits that her work and that of her colleagues "can, at least temporarily, leave us miserable, disempowered, bitter, and disappointed."

All of this leads to a basic if impertinent question: "Gee, Nanette, there are easier ways for talented lawyers to make lots more money. Why do you bother?"

She's bothering in order to repair the world, and she does so whenever she guides a young mother, unjustly separated from her children, through the bewildering bureaucratic maze that leads to family reunification. She repairs the world by encouraging other determined women through months-long odysseys of counseling, substance-abuse programs, and parenting classes that yield a new and hard-earned capacity to care for a child responsibly.

Not every story ends so successfully, of course. And sometimes Nanette is repairing the world most dramatically when she supports and represents parents who ultimately must make the painful decision to surrender their children for adoption. In those cases, Nanette is proclaiming by her work that even those who can't care properly for their own children are nonetheless dignified human beings. None of us is as bad as the worst thing we've ever done, or indeed, as bad as the bad things we cannot keep ourselves from doing. We're valuable not because of what we accomplish or how well we cope; we are valuable simply because we exist.

Each of us, whatever our livelihood, can repair the world by treating each person as equally dignified, whether he or she owns a bank, staffs the teller counter, or is too poor to open an account there. Doing so will transform our everyday encounters in taxis, supermarkets, or conference rooms; no longer mere opportunities to get something we want, these will become expressions of a spiritual purpose that pulls our life together and fills it with meaning.

Every once in a while, Nanette will run into some mother and child she has helped reunite. They may be walking hand in hand, shopping on one of those South Bronx streets, or stopping for lunch at a pizza parlor. The sight, unremarkable to the rest of us, is momentous for Nanette and the former client who greets her. Both of them know that life doesn't always turn out this way, and both have come to cherish this simplest of pleasures—mother and child hand in hand—that the rest of us take for granted. Such moments remind Nanette that she's not defending clients who wound up in terrible predicaments. Rather, she sees herself as "a defender of the right to love, helping parents and children find the opportunity to most fully express their love and care for one another."

And every time a parent and child "express their love and care for one another," wherever that may happen, our world has become a little more perfect.

Build the Civilization of Love

We are developing a strategy for life that will transform us and our world.

The first steps in that process were to figure out where we are and where we want to go. The next step was to understand our own purpose in the world. Both Nanette Schorr and Andrew Muras have looked at the world we've inherited and decided to lead it in a new direction. Andrew has come to understand that he is here on earth to be holy, and Nanette Schorr is here to repair the world.

And you?

Sixteenth-century Ignatius of Loyola opened his *Spiritual Exercises* by stating that we humans are created "to praise, reverence, and serve God." Ignatius didn't justify that statement, because he didn't have to. His audience, raised in relatively homogenous European Christendom, would have heard such statements from early childhood; listeners would have taken such words of human purpose for granted, whether or not they took them to heart.

But in a changing, culturally complex century, virtually nothing is taken for granted, including whether humans have a purpose at all. Truth is, we rarely think about that lofty question; we simply get on with our harried lives. As a result, we live in an "as if" culture. That is, some pursue wealth "as if" their purpose in life is to gather money. And others live as if they are here to pursue sex, to be entertained, to avoid boredom, or merely to show up every day at work and go home.

That style of living, as an earlier chapter showed, isn't working for us individually or for our civilization, hence the imperative to abandon "as if" living and embrace more intentionally purposeful living. We aren't living purposefully simply because we have jobs or classes to go to, or children and spouses to relate to. A worthy purpose must be mighty enough to lift us above our narrow everyday concerns, and it must be great enough to last a lifetime and cover a whole life—my purpose is not "just a job," even so worthy a role as banker, nurse, or parent.

I'm not inviting you to adopt Andrew's or Nanette's purpose, or even saintly Ignatius's. Each of us needs to find and speak words of purpose that resonate in our own hearts. Andrew and Nanette plumbed their deepest beliefs about the human person to frame their purposes. Likewise we ought to delve into our hearts and our spiritual beliefs to find in our purpose what Andrew and Nanette find in theirs: a connection between our spiritual beliefs and the work we do, a path to make our lives whole again, and a way to fill our work with greater meaning.

What is your mighty purpose?

What writings, beliefs, or experiences inspire your convictions about human purpose?

What legacy do you want to leave behind? What contribution to our civilization do you want to make through your life?

Discover Your Mighty Purpose

Evaluate the world you've inherited.
Envision the future worth fighting for.
Articulate a purpose worth living for.
» Embrace values worth standing for.
Put heart into strategy to give it life.

6

What Kind of Person Will You Be?

Embrace Values Worth Standing For

A recent U.S. presidential candidate ended up withdrawing from the race after a string of losses in early state primary elections. Vulture-like pundits had been circling his dying campaign for days and immediately swooped down to pick over its carcass. One commentator noted that people had considered this man "the perfect candidate"; his virtually unblemished résumé boasted noteworthy accomplishments over a long, distinguished, and varied career.

So what went wrong? Winning presidential candidates are usually so compelling that they have, in the pundit's words, "the ability to change people's minds." But this candidate "never got that far because he never failed to change his own mind first." Ouch. The campaign had fallen to pieces because "he had been too many things to too many people for too long."[1] Most pundits echoed the analysis, even if some voiced it more charitably. In essence, voters weren't completely sure that this candidate really knew who he was and what he stood for. He was presenting himself as a certain kind of person, but voters wondered whether he would be that same person two years after election day. They wondered whether he had any authentic core.

The criticisms may or may not have been fair. A political campaign is a nasty business in which operatives find an opponent's molehill-sized weaknesses and pile on the dirt until a mountain of doubt fills voters' minds.

Still, the pundits' fundamental point is indisputable: know who you are and know what you stand for. Be willing to stand for something over the long run if you hope to earn an authority so great as the presidency, a privilege so valuable as a friend's trust, or a quality so crucial as your own self-esteem.

This anecdote also illustrates what is and is not at the core of an authentic lifestyle in today's world. The candidate was criticized for allegedly changing his convictions. But voters were entirely unconcerned that he had also changed careers and residences multiple times during adulthood. That just shows how considerably the world has changed over the past twenty years. In the early 1980s, for example, J. P. Morgan colleagues and I might have looked slightly askance at a midcareer job candidate who had already worked at two or three different companies: What was wrong? Was he a poor performer who got bounced by his previous employers? Was she some flighty type who won't be dependable?

By the mid-1990s, however, our mind-set had swung 180 degrees: changing jobs had become so normal that we sometimes doubted midcareer candidates who had worked for only one company. Gee, why hasn't he sought out new opportunities before now? Maybe he's not good enough to get another job or not ambitious enough for what we need. Maybe she dislikes change and won't be able to adapt to our rapidly evolving business.

We've become used to a world of change. Most of us will change jobs and even careers more than once during a working lifetime. You may be single now, married later, and on your own once again later in life. You may be responsible only for yourself in young adulthood, then bring up children, and finally be cared for by those same children during your old age.

Which raises some questions: Who are you and what are you about? Is there anything that lasts through all that change? We've been erecting a foundation that will endure through change, including a vision of the world you want to help create and your purpose in bringing that world to be. Still, you'll be living out that purpose through multiple roles and multiple jobs. The key question on any one day may seem to be, What job will I do? But the key question throughout a whole lifetime is, What kind of person will I be?

Your values answer that question. Your values ultimately tell you (and others) who you are and what you are about as a person. Who you are amid life's twists and turns remains constant so long as your values do. Whether you are running for president or looking in your bathroom mirror, your values are your core.

Most of us are familiar with core values or values statements from our workplaces, and most of us frankly think those statements are a crock. Organizations talk the talk, but they don't walk the talk. Consider a 2002 *Business Week* survey, for example, where only 4 percent of professional investors were "very confident" that "corporations accurately report how much money they make."[2] All organizations talk about integrity, but apparently we don't believe they actually have any.

I polled a few friends, and each one shared the broader public skepticism. An army lieutenant told of a commander who issued troops a supplementary dog tag enumerating the army's values. But, my friend continued, "that was the beginning and the end of his value-based leadership; [it] came across as gimmicky and lacked credibility." A senior investment banker summed up the issue: "The reason people yawn when they hear [about missions and values] is that most companies are neither authentic nor practicing when it comes to values and purpose." Or, as he put it, "Core values are what we deeply believe in, not what we should believe in."

He's right. We need leaders who don't just mouth platitudes but who walk their talk. He rightly points out that *authentic* and *practicing* are the watchwords when it comes to values, and each of those words represents a different challenge.

Authenticity is the first test of my values and purpose. If I say I'm here on earth to repair the world or to be holy, do I really, really mean it? Do these ideas make me live and work differently, or do they ultimately hold no more significance than an empty slogan emblazoned across a glossy corporate annual report? Can I say that I'm here on earth for a reason, or am I simply drifting along, grasping after whatever suits a short-term need or a current fad?

If authenticity of purpose is the first test, then putting purpose into practice is the second and equally daunting challenge. For the loftier our purpose, the more we test our imagination to find everyday ways to demonstrate that purpose in how we live. I may be inspired enough to commit to building the civilization of love, but can I live that extraordinary-sounding purpose throughout life's very ordinary routines of commuting to work, answering office e-mail, keeping a house clean, balancing a checkbook, and doing chores?

Our values are the answer; they are the means by which we translate purpose into practice all day, every day. Three stories will show us values at work in three very different circumstances. An executive's nightmarish business crisis introduces integrity, a value for ourselves. A hospital administrator champions reverence, a value for others. And a high school teacher models excellence, a value for our work.

Integrity: A Value for Ourselves

Dave Collins spent virtually his whole professional career at Johnson & Johnson (J&J), the giant health-care company with near-iconic associations to childhood—baby powder, No More Tears baby shampoo, and Band-Aids.

So it wouldn't be very good for business if the company whose reputation rests squarely on safe products for our loved ones might be churning out products that killed people. Dave Collins and other J&J executives faced that horrific prospect on an October morning in 1982 when a Chicago reporter asked the company to comment on reports that someone had died after taking Tylenol, J&J's best-selling pain reliever.

It would later become clear that seven people had died after ingesting Tylenol capsules laced with cyanide by a deranged saboteur who restocked them on store shelves for purchase by unsuspecting customers. The stories proved both horrifying and poignant. One young girl awoke with a sore throat; her parents medicated her with Tylenol and, not long after, found their daughter dying on the bathroom floor. In another case, a twenty-seven-year-old man died after taking Tylenol. Distressed relatives converged on his home to comfort one another, baffled by the healthy young man's sudden death due to unknown causes. In a bitter twist of fate, two of the grieving relatives sought relief from tension headaches by taking Tylenol from their deceased relative's medicine chest—from the same tainted bottle. They, too, died.

But all those facts would become clear only days later, once company employees, coroners, and public-health officials had pieced together records from the sprawling, million-plus Chicagoland suburbs where the first death was reported. At the outset, Dave Collins, overseeing the division that manufactured Tylenol, had only a sketchy news report and questions of life-and-death import: Were consumers dying because of Tylenol? How had the problem happened? How widespread was it? What should be done about it?

A crisis team scrambled to assemble facts and immediately recalled Tylenol from Chicago-area store shelves. They quite quickly discovered that the defective Tylenol had been manufactured at four different times in two different factories, so it seemed almost impossible that manufacturing malfunctions or inside sabotage could have caused the tragedy. Rather, the product must have been tampered with after reaching Chicago store shelves. Within about twenty-four hours, exhausted company officials felt they were getting a grip on the crisis: the problem was apparently isolated to Chicago and had been contained thanks to the recall. They prepared to meet with Food and Drug Administration (FDA) officials

to explore the industrywide ramifications: dozens of similarly pack-
aged brands of medicine filled store shelves. Now that a previously
unimaginable act of sabotage had occurred, the industry would have
to pioneer completely new tamper-proof packaging.

But before that forward-looking meeting convened, J&J officials
were alerted to a new report of tainted Tylenol in the San Francisco
Bay Area. The report sounded dubious. (In fact, it turned out to
be a fraudulent extortion scheme). But company executives didn't
know that as they huddled to consider another crisis recall, this
time on the West Coast.

Their decision has since become a standard case study in business
ethics textbooks. The J&J executives neither waited to investigate
the dubious new tampering claim nor recalled Bay Area Tylenol.
Rather, they recalled every one of 30 million bottles of Tylenol
from every store shelf in the United States.

I lunched with Dave Collins to learn how J&J executives had
agonized over one of the most momentous decisions in the company's history. I wondered how they debated the trade-offs before
deciding on what was then the costliest recall ever in corporate
history. In fact, he didn't need a lunch hour to tell me; by the
time I'd finished a sip of water, he had finished recounting the
deliberations.

"Well, we had the credo," he said, "so there really was no choice."
End of story. He was referring to J&J's corporate value statement,
the credo, which begins: "We believe our first responsibility is to
the doctors, nurses and patients, to mothers and fathers and all
others who use our products and services. In meeting their needs
everything we do must be of high quality." So, on an October morning when facts were elusive, a handful of exhausted executives
agreed that a nationwide Tylenol recall was the "high-quality" way
to honor their credo's first responsibility to those who used their
products. That was it. No flip charts, no financial analysis of how
much the recall would cost, no what-ifs, and no assessment of the
possible negative ramifications for other J&J products. Just a gut
check on what they believed, followed by a quick decision. Some

executives undoubtedly figured that they were not just recalling their best-selling product but bidding it farewell forever.

As Dave sees it, the groundwork for their decision had been laid a few years earlier, when the newly anointed J&J chief executive James Burke launched a global series of "credo challenge" meetings with top managers. Dave explained that "the credo had been with us for decades, and Jim wanted to test whether it still stood up in modern times. He didn't want it to become some empty set of slogans. If we could no longer honor it because of changing business conditions, then he was open to changing it. But if we were going to keep it, he wanted it to be because managers had thought about it and decided they wanted to live by it." So team members were given the opportunity to challenge the credo and then change it, scrap it, or recommit to it.

By convening those meetings, J&J's chief executive had made things personal: from then on, no manager could regard the credo as some abstract values statement. Rather, each manager had to decide to own those values, or not. Recall an investment banker's earlier comment: "Core values are what we deeply believe in, not what we should believe in." The J&J managers got a chance to decide what they believed in, and they decided that they believed in their credo. Then, the ultimate credo challenge meeting occurred on that October morning when J&J's top executives had to decide whether they themselves really believed those values, too.

Companies don't believe in things; only human beings believe. The word *credo*, in fact, means "I believe" in Latin, and J&J's values—or any organization's values—are meaningful only when those who come to work each day take those values personally. People don't get their values from work; they bring their values to work. That's why the Tylenol story isn't, in the end, about a big company; it's a story about personal integrity, about sticking by the values we espouse, even when it's costly.

The dictionary defines *value* in two quite different ways, as a thing's "worth in money" or as something "desirable or worthy of esteem for its own sake."[3] If James Burke, Dave Collins, and their colleagues had wanted to put a price on their integrity, they would have found some way to appease the public and the FDA short of the drastic national recall. After all, only a few tainted capsules surfaced in only one region; it ultimately cost about $100 million to implement the massive recall, not to mention the $650 million that investors shaved from J&J's stock market value as the episode unfolded.

But they didn't perform those calculations. They didn't value their integrity for its worth in money. Rather, their integrity was worthy of esteem for its own sake. It wasn't for sale.

Weak people sell out their values when it's convenient or expedient. People with integrity, on the other hand, hang on to their values even when it's difficult or unpopular to do so. The root of the word *value* means "to be strong." People with integrity are strong themselves, and they consequently strengthen the rest of us. For that reason, they are also *valiant*, another word sharing that same Latin root.

Integrity, above all, is a value for ourselves. Recall its Latin root, which means "whole." Our integrity is what makes us the same people at work and at home, people who don't say one thing and do another. And because our word means the same today as it did yesterday, we see the same face in the mirror each morning and can be proud of the person we're looking at. Chances are, no one will die when we sacrifice our personal integrity, but we sacrifice some piece of ourselves when we do, and we face a diminished person in the mirror the following morning.

Reverence: A Value for Others

When you welcome newborns into this world and accompany the aged to death, you understand how humans ought to treat one another during the precious moments of life in between: with reverence.

That belief guides the seventy thousand or so nurses, administrators, doctors, and others who form Catholic Health Initiatives, a gutsy twentieth-century chapter of a gutsy nineteenth-century story.

Gutsy is not the first word one would have chosen for Maryanna Coyle, a gracious, soft-spoken woman who would have topped five feet tall only if she wore high heels (and Sr. Maryanna Coyle didn't wear those). Nor, for that matter, does *gutsy* spring to mind when regarding yellowing photos of Sr. Maryanna's wimple-shrouded nineteenth-century predecessors who helped shape the American frontier. We're familiar with the usual characters of America's westward expansion: prospectors, railroad builders, farmers, and rootless ne'er-do-wells who struck out to make fortunes, better their family's lot, or escape persecution in their home countries. We're less familiar with those in the pioneers' wake, among them countless nuns who provided the first organized, professional health care and education to myriad frontier towns.

Stories of the sisters' pluck abound. A drunken prospector once spat on Sister of Providence Mother Joseph as she begged for money for the orphanages and clinics she founded across the Pacific Northwest. Her reply: "OK. That was for me. Now give me something for these children." She and other pioneer sisters had to be pretty thick-skinned when it came to raising money. Franciscan lore, for example, celebrates a band of sisters sent out to open a hospital with a grand total of $2. The hospital still stands, as do some dozen more hospitals that the congregation founded. Pardon the expression, but these tough dames could make $2 go a long way.

Their successors proved equally resourceful in the late twentieth century amid very different challenges. The evolving health-care industry threatened to decimate the patchwork of small hospitals the earlier sisters had founded. Massive for-profit hospital chains were gobbling up independent hospitals. Most religious orders, in contrast, were running smaller hospital systems and lacked the purchasing power and other benefits of scale that the hospital conglomerates enjoyed. The sisters' hospital systems consequently faced financial ruin, and economies of scale weren't their only woe: the sisters' ranks had plummeted: in the mid-1960s there were some 180,000 nuns in the United States; today there are about 70,000.[4]

Sr. Maryanna and her lay colleagues faced a bleak future of ever-diminishing spiritual influence on hospital systems that were slowly drifting toward bankruptcy. To survive, they accomplished what few others would have dared to conceive of: uniting separate hospital systems sponsored by various religious orders into one health-care network that could thrive in the long run and protect its spiritual identity. Imagine the complexity of unraveling and reassembling legal structures, technology platforms, and human resources policies. It's maddeningly difficult to put two companies together; try doing that with five companies. But instead of investment bankers and cigar-chomping corporate executives huddled at conference tables, picture Franciscans, Sisters of Charity, Sisters of Mercy, other nuns, and their lay colleagues trying to engineer one of the health-care industry's most complicated mergers ever.

Anyone who has engineered a merger (or merely survived one) knows that team spirit and shared purpose can be trampled in the urgent push to complete a deal. A conglomerate emerges that everyone hopes will be financially stronger. But sometimes the cost is a company's sense of soul, and "I'm proud to work there" gives way to "It's just a job."

Even a bevy of nuns risk losing their souls (pardon the expression) in the course of pulling off a big merger, and such concerns preoccupied Sr. Maryanna as she and her colleagues attended another of countless meetings to sort through merger details. A working group was presenting the new organization's draft values statement, the sort of thing that weary management teams typically nod at before moving on to "more important" things—that is, financial concerns. The draft statement was uncontroversial; respect headed the proposed set of values. Of course respect headed the list. What else would you expect of a hospital system run by nuns?

Well, something more than respect, apparently. Sr. Maryanna halted the proceedings and asked her colleagues to recall why they were in the health-care business. Nineteenth-century nuns, many of them immigrants, hadn't left homelands and families to traverse a harsh frontier because they merely respected those they would serve. Something stronger drove them: reverence. And so, from that afternoon, one of the world's largest hospital networks has stood for "reverence: profound respect and awe for all of creation . . . our relationships with others and our journey to God."

The dictionary tells us that reverence is "a feeling or attitude of deep respect, love, and awe, as for something sacred."[5] Anyone who has ever held a newborn baby or a dying relative's hand knows that feeling of reverence. It's easy enough to imagine how reverence might vitalize doctors and nurses, but I wondered how the hospitals' lawyers and kitchen staff, for example, connected this very spiritual value to their very worldly occupations. I knew I could find reverence in a delivery room, but what about an office cubicle? The hospital network talked the talk, but how could it (or the rest of us, for that matter) walk the talk of reverence in everyday occupations?

Well, we can learn about walking the talk by walking across the hospital lobby floor that Charles Bynum cleans and polishes every day at Memorial Health Care System in Chattanooga, Tennessee. If a previous chapter gave us Sr. Saturnina walking up and down Caracas hills every day, this chapter gives us Charles Bynum on level ground, meticulously guiding his buffing machine in graceful arcs, up and down the length of a lobby floor.

One day, while tending another of his cleanup duties, he overheard a hospital visitor telling her husband that the lobby floors "have a shine where you can see yourself. I can see the bottom of my feet as I walk across them, and it reminds me of Christ walking on water."

The woman later complimented Bynum's boss, who passed the word back to him. Here's how Charles Bynum sums it up: "I'm grateful to have a ministry that touches lives as I shine floors."

Lots of us occasionally doubt that our work makes any difference in others' lives. Yet "just" by shining floors, Charles Bynum managed to free someone, at least temporarily, from anxiety and stress over her own illness or that of a loved one. Imagine if we all worked in ways that made our customers and colleagues feel as if they were walking on water. Imagine if we all cleaned up floors and spreadsheets and babies' behinds and legal disputes in ways that made others feel as special as that woman did. Surely the word *reverence* is the right word for that "feeling or attitude of deep respect, love, and awe, as for something sacred." In the book of Genesis, God says, "Let us make humankind in our image, according to our likeness" (1:26). Charles Bynum is shining floors as if he believes we're all made in God's image.

Excellence: A Value for Our Work

Charles Bynum's reverence of others becomes clear through his excellent work, and he previews our third value: we owe integrity to ourselves, reverence to others, and excellence to all that we do. As Ecclesiastes tells us, "Whatever your hand finds to do, do with your might" (9:10). Steve Duffy epitomized this attitude.

Fr. Duffy taught high school students for fifty-six years. That may not be a record, but it must be close. He got around to me in 1972, my first year in high school and his twenty-seventh (give or take) of teaching. We intimidated fourteen-year-olds beheld this gaunt, gray-haired, stoop-shouldered old man much as Israelites must have regarded their imposing (and unwelcome) prophets. He looked a few weeks shy of the embalmer's table, and none of us would have bet Duffy still had thirty years of life left, much less thirty years of teaching.

We didn't bet on his life span, but we did lots of betting nevertheless. Duffy was the consummate racketeer for good causes, regularly roaming the school cafeteria inducing gullible fourteen-year-olds to shell out a dime apiece on his weekly pro-football betting pool (the week's winner took home half the proceeds; Duffy allocated the rest to projects that served impoverished developing world communities). When not luring kids to gamble on football, Duffy pursued other dubious extracurricular activities, like scouring subway cars for advertising posters that might enliven a Latin or religion class. When he found a suitable poster, I guess he stole it. (He claimed that he sought the transit authority's permission, but I'm not sure he bothered. People were shooting one another in New York subways back then; who was going to arrest an old man in a Roman collar for pinching a cardboard advertisement?)

Duffy had taught Latin for decades, but fifty-plus years of its unchanging conjugations weren't enough to sate his appetite for them; he devoted after-school hours to patiently tutoring the kids who weren't understanding those conjugations and declensions that he had already taught a few thousand times in his long career.

He also taught religion, treating startled freshmen early on to an appallingly bad rendition of a *Porgy and Bess* song: "the things that you're liable to read in the Bible, they ain't necessarily so." It was shocking to hear a priest say so, but that's how Duffy taught high school freshmen that biblical passages must often be interpreted rather than read literally, because their inspired authors sometimes used literary forms like poetry and storytelling to convey their revealed message.[6]

He was teaching sophisticated ideas, but his religion classes seemed easy. He handed out custom-made mimeographed sheets summarizing each lesson's key points. Even kids who couldn't master Latin could salvage self-esteem with an A in religion. In fact, by senior year, Duffy himself seemed too easy. Although he was ever beloved, his antics seemed better suited to high school freshmen than to us eighteen-year-old sophisticates.

A few years later, while studying an upper-level college text on the Old Testament, I learned who had, or had not, been sophisticated back in high school. Déjà vu plagued me, chapter after chapter, until I tracked down Duffy's mimeographed notes from a pack-rat friend who, for some reason, had saved his high school religion notebooks. The parallels were unmistakable. Duffy's mimeographed notes were based on that text. He had taught college-level theology to fourteen-year-olds and made the material seem easy.

We might think of star athletes as examples of human excellence, but their "excellence" springs from a superabundance of natural gifts— no matter how hard you or I work, we won't throw ninety-seven-mile-an-hour fastballs or slam dunk basketballs. But we can all excel as Duffy did. Good enough is pacing students through a textbook's pages; excellence is riding subway cars in imaginative pursuit of something that will spark greater, more excited insight. Good enough is coasting on your natural teaching talent (God knows Duffy had plenty); excellence is developing and honing your talents for five decades. Here's how St. Augustine captured the spirit of excellence that so obviously drove Duffy: "I will suggest a means whereby you can praise God all day long, if you wish. Whatever you do, do it well, and you have praised God."[7] The Muslim tradition expresses the same idea even more succinctly: God "loves, when one of you is doing something, that he [or she] do it in the most excellent manner."[8]

Devotees of human excellence develop not only their own talent but also the talent of those they touch. Duffy's commitment to excellence kindled his seemingly absurd belief that kids could understand college-level theology if it were pitched to them appropriately. We did understand it, because his excellence coaxed ours to blossom. The Latin root of *excel* conveys the sense of rising out of or rising above. That's what excellence is: rising above ourselves, and lifting up those around us, by getting the most from our talents and gifts.

In a short essay written not long before his death, Duffy spoke about the way he dealt with high school students: "I see myself radiating Christ to my students at all times. . . . I do this by my concern and love and respect for them. . . . I do it by being friendly in my dealings with them . . . [I think of Jesus] traveling with his companions, being with them twenty-four hours a day, and always having an effect on them by the way he dealt with them."[9]

That essay was Duffy's last lesson to us, one about absorbing and imparting values. He didn't write: "I read that Jesus told us to be compassionate, so I tell the students to be compassionate." Rather, Duffy imaginatively followed Jesus around, saw how Jesus treated his colleagues, and led his own life accordingly. Duffy saw Jesus "being with [his colleagues] twenty-four hours a day, and always having an effect on them by the way he dealt with them," and Duffy likewise devoted himself to having an effect, all day and every day, on the fellow travelers he taught, lived with, or worked beside.

Duffy (and the others profiled in this chapter) have found ways to express profoundly spiritual values through their very worldly work in classrooms, hospitals, and corporate offices. It's vital that we do the same if our life strategy is to succeed. After all, work is the pervasive human experience: though only 60 percent of adults may work for pay, all of us work—we do household chores, look after our children, prepare meals, tend gardens, and volunteer at churches or civic organizations. Work absorbs the largest share of our waking lives, often an overwhelming share when we factor in long commutes. Our strategy won't succeed if we can't connect what we consider ultimately important to what we do all day; we will inevitably be left feeling as if we are leading split lives.

Every religious and spiritual tradition imparts a vision of why humans are here on earth and how they ought to live and treat one another. And every tradition bids its adherents to make that vision central to their lives. Duffy did so by centering his life and work on human values that, for him, had deeply religious roots. At one level, he was teaching kids Latin, cajoling them into betting pools for charity, and figuring out how to sharpen his pedagogical skills. But at a deeper level, in all those same acts, he was drawing on his spiritual beliefs to be mindful of Jesus traveling with his companions, of being with them twenty-four hours a day, and of always having an effect on them.

Which raises a question: Jesus embodied many worthy values, and he famously extolled the meek, the merciful, and the peacemakers in his sermon on the mount. Why, then, were integrity, reverence, and excellence alone featured in this chapter? Come to think of it, shouldn't any master list of human values also include ideals like justice, courage, wisdom, and moderation, championed by the great Aristotle?

Well, it's not about the list, whether that list is authored by Aristotle, Confucius, Ignatius, or Jesus. It's about who you will be and how you will live. Consult your deepest beliefs, to be sure, but then consult your own heart and decide what kind of person you want to be. You have a brief journey on this planet—how will you treat yourself, your work, and those you meet along the way? If you treat yourself with integrity, your work with excellence, and those you meet with reverence, I suspect that you will end up manifesting plenty of other values that would make both Jesus and Aristotle proud.

Duffy figured out what other great leaders eventually understand: your most eloquent values statement is your example. Your personal, church, family, or organizational values are not what you say or print in a brochure, but how you treat people, how you run meetings, whom you hire, how you treat your child who wants to play when you come home exhausted, whether you inconvenience yourself to support your friends, and how you react in a host of other daily moments that, taken together, create your eloquent (or unimpressive) values statement. As Mahatma Gandhi once put it, "Be the change you want to see in the world."

What are some of the qualities of the people you most admire?

If someone followed you around for a typical week, what values would they say you embody?

What traits do you want to pass on to your children? What values do you want to stand for?

Evaluate the world you've inherited.
Envision the future worth fighting for.
Articulate a purpose worth living for.
Embrace values worth standing for.
» Put heart into strategy to give it life.

7

What Makes the Difference?

Put Heart into Strategy to Give It Life

N ow we must face a hard truth: even the best strategy won't work unless pursued with fierce will and courageous commitment. Put differently, our strategy comes fully alive only when we put our heart into it.

We saw heart-filled strategy in the Tylenol story, for example, when executives courageously followed policy that put customers' well-being before profit-and-loss margins. And we see a devastating lack of heart in the paradox of Christians who profess a common Father yet savagely butcher, enslave, marginalize, or neglect their brothers and sisters. Gandhi summons us to the great-heartedness that will be this chapter's focus: "Be the change you want to see in the world."

Talking about the heart of strategy may sound like romantic nonsense in a book about making major choices and getting results in a complicated world. But whether in business circles or in personal efforts to live well, few challenges are as great as the bundle of problems we'll call "putting your heart into your strategy." Some highly respected commentators on corporate America will help us frame the problem, and Ignatius of Loyola will help us resolve it.

Lacking the Courage
to Live as We Ought

If good ideas or brilliant plans guaranteed success, then plenty of defunct companies would still be in business. Thousands of companies go bankrupt annually, and many tens of thousands of individuals fall badly short of their personal aspirations. In many cases, these failed companies and individuals had every skill they needed for success. Moreover, they often knew what they had to accomplish and boasted fancy strategies with all the right ideas—what we might call the "head" part of strategy. They knew what they wanted to accomplish and where they wanted to go, but they lacked the courage and commitment to go there.

In a provocative 1995 article, the renowned Harvard Business School professor John Kotter investigated why transformation efforts fail. He was intrigued and worried that so many efforts to turn around sick companies—or to make average ones great— never seemed to work. Why was that? After all, smart management teams often labored for months over corporate turnaround plans, analyzed the business environment perceptively, and crafted bullet-proof strategies. But despite flawless planning, the turnarounds never happened, nor did the leap from so-so performance to excellence. Kotter prescribed various cures for management teams and other turnaround doctors, but his and other good advice notwithstanding, turnaround efforts are still failing in abundance: *Harvard Business Review* reprinted that very same article, word for word, a decade later.[1]

So business pundits are now searching out deeper-rooted explanations. They are looking less at techniques and tactics and a lot more closely at attitudes and beliefs. That's why, for example, *Harvard Business Review* has recently been concerned not only with the nuts and bolts of finance and management but also with "courage as a skill" and "discovering your authentic leadership," to cite just two recent article titles.[2] Similarly, widely consulted management commentator Peter Senge points out in *The Fifth Discipline*, "Real commitment is still rare in today's organizations. It is our experience that 90% of the time, what passes for commitment is compliance."[3] Too many folks are going through the motions with little passion or deep interest in their work.

These respected commentators are diagnosing symptoms that point to a common malady. Whether in politics, business, or our religious institutions—whether in our professional or in our personal lives—only with courage and character will we surmount the vexing problems that life throws at us. Great ideas and great strategies don't suffice; we also need to be great hearted and great spirited. For example, a former presidential aide described his profound disillusionment at working in a White House that boasted lofty ideals but lacked the spirit to pursue them: "That same passion for the poor I first heard [from the president] was in his voice and in his eyes. But the passion was a passion for talking about compassion, not fighting for compassion."[4] Former President Bill Clinton diagnosed the missing ingredient even more starkly: "Most of us don't have the courage to live the way we ought."[5] Most poignantly, South African freedom fighter and former president Nelson Mandela once reflected that, throughout years of cruel internment at the harsh Robben Island detention camp, "My greatest enemy was not those who put or kept me in prison. It was myself. I was afraid to be who I am."

This book has been laying out a strategy, and a closer look at the word illuminates the vital ingredient that brings it to life. The word *strategy* combines two ancient Greek roots: *stratos* ("army") and *agein* ("to lead"). So strategy originally concerned what one did to lead the army well. For example, a general can't lead the army well without developing and communicating a mission, nor can we lead our own lives well without a similarly clear sense of purpose.

But while good strategy may begin with using our heads to articulate a worthy mission, it culminates in our hearts, with qualities like commitment, inspiration, persistence, authenticity, and courage. Leadership is not just knowing who we want to be but also finding the courage to become that person, whether heading our country, our company, or our own family. Making strategy requires a good head, but making strategy happen requires a great heart.

The astute commentators quoted earlier have accurately diagnosed the deficit of courage and authenticity that increasingly hobbles efforts to transform our lives, companies, or countries; but those experts have been less adept at prescribing solutions. They have not really explained how we make ourselves great hearted and great spirited.

Qualities of the heart have always been crucial ingredients of a life successfully lived; the issue is not particular to our time, even if it's grown more acute. And it is not to a contemporary that we turn, now, for help with our hearts and spirits, but to sixteenth-century Ignatius of Loyola, whose life story and Spiritual Exercises will point a path toward greater-hearted living.

A Saint Who Put
Head and Heart Together

Ignatius of Loyola was born in 1491 in Spain's Basque region. While medieval peasants learned peaceable resignation to their meager status in life, minor nobles like Ignatius restlessly pursued advancement. A court apprenticeship at the age of fourteen broadened his social network, refined his practice of chivalry, honed his military skills, and—so his biographers suggest—enabled him to chase women. A decade or so later, while defending a military outpost at Pamplona, his first great opportunity for military glory arrived when French invaders did.

He fought valiantly but suffered ignominious defeat. An enemy cannonball shattered Ignatius's leg and, with it, his military career. He was stretchered home over miles of bumpy dirt trails. His crudely set fracture didn't heal properly, leaving an unsightly protrusion. The medieval version of orthopedic surgeons hacked away at the protruding bone (imagine what passed for medieval anesthesia). Loyola lived, which was a better-than-average result for the barbaric surgery he had endured. But he limped along forever after, one visibly deformed leg shorter than the other.

His autobiography recounts convalescent days filled with idle daydreaming, which eventually led to more purposeful daydreaming. Fantasies of chivalrous glory receded as fantasies of religious service began percolating. Ignatius described a newly emerging identity*: "The greatest consolation I experienced was gazing at the sky and the stars, which I often did and for long, because I thus felt within myself a very great impulse to serve our Lord."[6]

That powerful urge spurred a pietistic, haphazardly implemented pilgrimage to the Holy Land, punctuated by a stopover at the Spanish town of Manresa, where powerful mystical experiences so intensified Ignatius's religious convictions and devotion that, as he put it later in life, "even if I gathered up all the various helps I may have had from God and all the various things I have known, even adding them all together, I do not think I got as much as at that one time."[7]

It's fortunate that Ignatius's religious commitment had become so unwaveringly intense, for he needed whatever internal strength he could muster to get through the near-continuous setbacks that filled his early postconversion years: jail terms, sickness, suicidal impulses, crippling self-doubt, and months invested in a futile dream to live in the Holy Land.

Penniless and virtually directionless after being forced to leave the Holy Land, Loyola recalls, "ponder[ing] within myself what I ought to do; and eventually I was rather inclined to study for some time so I would be able to help souls."[8] At the age of thirty-four, he faced the brutal fact that he was not well-enough educated to help souls as he aspired. He had searched for—and was finally beginning

---

*Ignatius refers to himself in the third person throughout his autobiography; for ease of understanding, all quotes have been transformed into first-person.

to find—a way to translate his spiritual beliefs into a real-world purpose: I'm here on earth "to help souls." The onetime military commander prepared for that new purpose from a humbling low rung: sitting in a grammar school alongside little children so that he could complete remedial studies in Latin.

Most biographers chronicle what might be considered Ignatius's triumphs. He learned basic grammar (and a lot more), eventually studying at medieval Europe's most prestigious academic institution, the University of Paris. There he befriended Francis Xavier and other colleagues who were ordained as priests and together founded in 1540 what remains the world's largest fully integrated religious company—the Society of Jesus, better known as the Jesuits—now active in more than one hundred countries. During the early years of their history, Jesuits helped develop the modern calendar and the Vietnamese alphabet, negotiate the Russian–Chinese border, and found one of the world's largest cities, São Paolo.

But we're less interested in stories of Jesuit corporate success than in understanding Ignatius's personal transformation and what it might teach us about finding the courage and commitment to become inspired leaders of our own lives.

We certainly find in Loyola all the courage and will that any of us would need to conquer our own respective challenges. He plowed ahead resolutely despite disappointments and setbacks. After his battle injury shattered his career aspirations, he pulled his life back together and set off on a months-long, countries-wide odyssey of personal discovery. Well into middle age, when his noble peers would have been enjoying their peak influence and prestige, Ignatius was swallowing his pride to retool his skills in a grammar school classroom. Although church officials wrongly jailed and harassed him, he persevered in serving his church. Late in life, at an age when his peers were winding down their productive years, he took the entrepreneurial gambit of starting the Jesuits against very long odds of success.

How do the rest of us find such courage, perseverance, and strength of will? We find a few clues by examining Ignatius's life in light of contemporary studies about leadership. For example, his life pattern seems to vindicate what the professors Warren Bennis and Robert Thomas reported after interviewing numerous business and public-sector leaders, namely, that many "had endured intense and often traumatic experiences that transformed them. . . . The skills required to conquer adversity and emerge stronger and more committed than ever are the same ones that make extraordinary leaders."[9] Jim Collins drew similar conclusions about some of the outstanding leaders profiled in *Good to Great*, noting that a personal crisis or some "significant life experience . . . might have sparked or furthered their maturation."[10]

The Harvard emeritus psychologist Abraham Zaleznik helped us understand why. "Leaders," he once wrote, "are 'twice born' individuals who endure major events that lead to a sense of separateness, or perhaps estrangement, from their environments. As a result, they turn inward in order to return with a created rather than an inherited sense of identity"—exactly as Ignatius did.[11] Imagine the identity crisis that must have afflicted the macho, vain Ignatius of Loyola after finding himself transformed overnight into a deformed, limping creature: surely it was a profound assault to his inherited sense of identity.

Or, more vividly, consider another injured soldier-turned-leader, Robert Dole, who later became a U.S. senator and the Republican Party's 1996 presidential candidate. During a World War II battle, Dole's body had been shredded by waves of machine-gun fire as he led a platoon up a hillside to attack a well-defended enemy trench. Years later, he recalled the weeks immediately following that injury. "On good days, I could move a finger or arm a little; on bad days, I struggled to move at all. I felt imprisoned in my frozen body. I still could not control my bladder or bowels."[12]

The names of Ignatius of Loyola and Bob Dole may never before have appeared in the same sentence, but despite different centuries and different professions, they teach a common lesson: the journey to a new empowered sense of self often involves relinquishing some former sense of who we are, why we matter, and what our lives are about. The injured Bob Dole who couldn't control his bladder and relied on nurses to diaper him surely realized that he was not the man he once thought he was. Many people never recover from that painful realization, whether occasioned by bodily injury, bankruptcy, school failure, family breakup, being fired, or hundreds of other ego-shattering traumas.

Yet for countless others, the destruction of our sense of self is prelude to a personal resurrection of sorts, which is the second part of the dynamic that Zaleznik observed. That is, the crisis breaks down the inherited sense of self and spurs a passage to a new, empowering, created sense of identity. Here's how the mature Bob Dole recalled his own transformational moment—his embrace of new purpose—during convalescence: "I came close to dying three times, facing death and living to tell about it. Why was I still alive? Maybe there was some bigger meaning to my life. Maybe there was something more that I was meant to do."[13]

There is a larger meaning—to everyone's life. In the chapters leading up to this one, we were challenged to articulate that larger meaning—our mighty purpose and clear vision of a better world. Unfortunately, though, reading this book won't be enough to ignite deep-in-the-gut courage and commitment to pursue our mighty purpose through the distractions, tribulations, discouragements, and hardships that fill an ordinary life.

In fact, stories of Ignatius and Bob Dole might leave us feeling even further from a solution than we were before. Personal crisis can be a leadership crucible, as it was for both Dole and Ignatius. But what are the rest of us to do—wait around for a crisis? We can't count on going through trauma such as warfare, and we wouldn't wish trauma on others or ourselves.

After all, Ignatius's story isn't what you would label a "strategic initiative"; what he went through was a conversion experience. *Conversion* is an intimidating word, one we narrowly associate with an intellectual decision to adopt a certain religious creed, as in, "He converted to Catholicism." But conversion involves a richer, more profound, and more comprehensive transformation: the word's Latin roots suggest a decisive "turn" from one way of life to another. Whether or not a change of religious belief is involved, conversion can describe any decision to turn from self-destructive addictions or behaviors, self-indulgence, moral degeneracy, hopelessness, or fear—combined with a turn toward a more purposeful life characterized by an empowering and hopeful vision of the future.

Each of us needs such a turn to succeed in our strategies. Unless we are transformed people, we won't summon the will and courage to pursue the demands of a truly great vision. But such turning is part mystery; we don't completely know how to transform others or ourselves into deeply courageous and strong-willed people, just as we don't quite understand why some people rebound resiliently from crises while others are crushed by them.

We can't manufacture conversion or solve completely the mystery behind the great-heartedness that transforms strategy into reality. But we do find, in contemporary research and in the spiritual wisdom of Ignatius, three distinct actions that can help lead us to bigger and braver hearts.

- Take it personally.
- Get over yourself.
- Go to your God.

Do you know people whose life direction and sense of commitment seem to have been transformed in the course of some crisis or difficult experience? What happened, and what do you think went on inside them?

Have you confronted personal pain, setbacks, challenges, or great joy? What did it do to you?

Take It Personally

A battle injury is not an abstraction; it's intense and searing. It's not a crisis; it's my crisis. Our strategies won't work unless we're as intensely and personally invested in them as Ignatius and Dole must have been in their transformative experiences.

I served on more than one management task force charged with being wordsmiths for the finer points of a departmental or organizational strategy. We would polish our product, distribute well-articulated strategic plans, and soon end up wondering why our subordinates didn't get it or buy into the new direction. After all, we ourselves were fired up about the ideas; why weren't the rest of them? Well, we were operating as if the key to switching on our teams and subordinates were a winning piece of logic or a finely turned phrase. But what had fired us up was the process of thinking through the strategy, arguing over it, choosing its words carefully, and taking pride in our output. In other words, the strategy worked for us because it was our work. We took it personally. Words, ideas, and strategies make a difference not because they are well phrased, but because we come to believe them deeply.

Ignatius of Loyola understood the distinction. On the one hand, his *Exercises* open with an unambiguous articulation of human purpose: we "are created to praise, reverence, and serve God" (#23). But of the hundred or so pages of exercises, only a few paragraphs elaborate that purpose statement. He is obviously less interested in teaching about a purpose than in provoking us to internalize a purpose. As the Jesuit theologian Walter Burghardt once explained, "The exercises are not primarily an intellectual enterprise; from beginning to end they are an experience. Ignatius asks me to walk with the Jesus of Nazareth, talk with the Jesus of Jerusalem."[14]

That's why the exercises allow no casual bystanders or disinterested readers. Ignatius pushes participants into the middle of virtually every meditation. Remember how we began to work out strategy in this book: we took stock of the world we've inherited, including the injustice of young children crawling around Manila garbage dumps. But we didn't walk the garbage dump ourselves; we gazed at it from a safe distance. Maybe we attributed such miseries to inept local governments or to the fallout of a rapidly globalizing economy.

Ignatius's exercises likewise begin by taking stock of the world around us, but Ignatius does not allow us to turn all the world's suffering and sinfulness into someone else's responsibility. Rather, we must also take stock of the part we've played, for good and ill, in getting the world to where it stands. Ignatius counsels us to "ask for shame and confusion about myself, when I see . . . how many times I have deserved eternal damnation for my many sins" (#48). How's that for taking things personally!

But shame is prelude to equally intense wonder and awe that, whatever our inadequacies, we are still here. Ignatius invites us to "an exclamation of wonder and surging emotion" that we're alive. And not just alive but graced and privileged; a later exercise urges us to ponder the miracle of our humanity: "I will consider how God dwells . . . in human beings, giving them intelligence; and finally, how in this way he dwells also in myself, giving me existence, life, sensation, and intelligence; and even further, making me his temple, since I am created as a likeness and image of the Divine Majesty" (#235).

The incredible miracle that you are here at all, and much less are a dignified, talented person, will almost invariably lead you to conclude that you must be here for a reason. As you ponder your life, its purpose, and your values, take it personally. This is not a mental game—there is bigger meaning to your life. You are unique, and your actions have consequence in the world.

Get Over Yourself

But now the process becomes tricky. Bigger meaning is necessarily something bigger than ourselves, and we can't grab hold of purpose greater than ourselves without letting go of our ego obsession. We won't be visionary if we can't see beyond the tips of our own noses. The very opening sentence of the evangelist Rick Warren's best-selling *The Purpose-Driven Life* lays it out plainly: "It's not about you."[15] Or as we New Yorkers might put it: get over yourself.

We cannot pursue great purpose passionately and doggedly unless we care deeply, take it very personally, and become fully invested in what we're doing. But when we invest wholeheartedly in a purpose, we sometimes turn ourselves into the purpose—I did this, I accomplished this, I'm saving the world, others need to buy into my vision. Anyone who has worked alongside ambitious colleagues in a big company has seen the type. But most of us have also lived and worked alongside great leaders—including great spouses, parents, priests, and teachers—who managed both to care deeply and to get over themselves. In *Good to Great*, Jim Collins finds just such qualities in leaders who seem to be "a study in duality: modest and willful, humble and fearless." Or, as he later describes them, "a paradoxical mix of personal humility and professional will."[16]

Go to Your God

To be honest, I don't know how to live out that paradox of qualities—modest and willful, humble and fearless. Neither do I understand how conversion happens, that profound and energized turn from what is self-destructive to what is life giving. Some, like Ignatius of Loyola, seem to get over themselves and turn to new life after seeing themselves in pieces. Others seem to get there in some powerfully graced moment: facing the death of a loved one, witnessing the birth of a child, experiencing natural beauty in an intense way, or experiencing revulsion just as intensely when seeing the natural world destroyed and humans in misery.

A man I barely knew once told me about the defining turn in his own life trajectory. One afternoon, well into adulthood, he attended a healing service at which a community prayed for its aging and ailing members, his parents included. He quite unexpectedly found himself reeling, his focus ping-ponging between the many frail elderly and his own weighty preoccupations as a father, breadwinner, and, apparently, a hell-raiser.

That night, he knelt down beside his bed and prayed. "I hadn't done that in years," he told me. "For me, praying at bedtime was something you did when you were a little kid. I don't know why I did it; the healing service had thrown me off balance somehow." Here was the totality of his prayer: "God, I don't know. I do lots of bad things, and I don't think I can stop doing them." He didn't tell me what those bad things were, but his nose looked as if it might have been busted once or twice, and his thick forearms and hands convinced me that he probably got the best of whatever drunken mayhem he had instigated over the years. He told me that from the morning following his bedside prayer his "desire to do those bad things slowly started to float away." He couldn't explain to me exactly what had happened or how. Neither could I explain it for him, or even relate to his experience. I (and many readers, I suspect) have never experienced such an obviously transformative moment.

Yet we keep moving. I recall a moment during a weeks-long walking trek across Spain. At the end of one long day, some two dozen of us sweaty, dirty, bedraggled pilgrims gathered in a west-of-nowhere rural church. Some trekkers were devout Christians, others were searching for spiritual meaning, and still others didn't quite know what they were seeking in that trek or even in their lives. The priest read a boilerplate prayer for our continued safety, then closed his prayer book and improvised: "I know you are hot and tired. But keep going. If you are looking for peace, you will find peace. If you are looking for God, God will find you."

We appreciated his hopeful promise because, frankly, most of us didn't feel any better, much less transformed, for having walked day after day through Spain's unforgiving summer. We mostly felt hot and tired. Yet we persevered in walking toward our goal, just as so many others persevere nobly despite little encouragement and difficult circumstances. Their lives have not been dramatically transformed in the fury of a crisis, by the blessing of unexpected great joy, or by the heavy burden of unanticipated sorrow. Yet I see evidence of hearts transformed in the lives of many who may not feel very transformed as they struggle forward. I think of a single mother who daily exhausts herself cleaning hotel rooms for near minimum wage, then comes home and somehow finds the energy to treat her children patiently and kindly. I know a teacher, underpaid to begin with, who regularly and ungrudgingly reaches into his own pocket to buy supplies that his school can't provide. I've seen store clerks treat with genuine respect those haughty customers who addressed them more harshly than they do their pet animals. I've met women whose families earn less than $2 a day, who have no real hope of earning more, who live in drug-ridden, unsanitary, violence-plagued slums—yet they pursue their children's education with the same perseverance and pride of mothers in America's wealthiest school districts.

I think of so many who remain dedicated to jobs, causes, families, and friends even when they are not fairly rewarded, can't see clear results, are overlooked, taken advantage of, or find no encouragement. I think of Mother Teresa, who persevered even while feeling, month after month after month, as if "there is such a terrible darkness within me, as if everything was dead. It has been like this more or less from the time I started 'the work'" of caring for Calcutta's indigent and dying.[17] Our most courageous of all may be all those people who simply manage to keep going even though they don't feel very courageous or transformed at all.

How do they find the strength to do so? "Be bold, and mighty forces will come to your aid," a nineteenth-century pastor once said. And surely it's boldness enough to keep trying to be holy when you are sorely tempted and distracted, to be reverent toward others even as they are treating you like s—t, to believe that the world can be better for your children even though they are being raised in a hellhole, or to remain committed to doing excellent work when no one recognizes it. I do believe that somehow, as all these every-day heroes struggle through trying and often unjust circumstances, mighty forces are coming to their aid, even when we, their brothers and sisters, are not.

What are those mighty forces? We all profess varying beliefs about the nature of this universe, the source of ultimate meaning, and whether we can commune with God, a higher power, or what-ever concept our respective traditions employ. I happen to believe, as that west-of-nowhere priest did, that "if you are looking for God, God will find you." Ignatius of Loyola or Mother Teresa would have likewise believed that even as we are looking, and even when we mostly feel lost, God is somehow finding us, whether or not it feels that way to us. Ignatius believed (as I do) that when we set ourselves toward some worthy purpose that transcends our meager strength, we tap into a source of meaning, strength, peace, and courage that is beyond us. We come to realize, in a graced moment, that we are called to some great purpose, that we cannot do it on our own, but that we don't have to do it on our own. That's why Ignatius urges, in one after another of his Spiritual Exercises, that we speak to Jesus "in the way one friend speaks to another, or a servant to one in authority—now begging a favor, now accusing oneself of some misdeed, now telling one's concerns and asking counsel about them" (#54).

I know that talk of conversion and transformation may seem out of place in this strategy for the worldly business of managing our lives and careers. But I also know that no ambitious strategy, personal or corporate, will succeed without courage and will. And anyone who thinks they will produce courage and will through a checklist, textbook, or seminar is either kidding themselves or sell-ing snake oil to the rest of us.

We recoil from acknowledging, in our often too-antiseptic boardrooms or statehouses, that great purpose and profound values are fundamentally spiritual, whether they are pursued in business, church, home, or politics. I cannot count the value of respect as I can count my possessions; nor can I prove the conviction that all of us are equal as I can prove a mathematical formula; nor can I touch integrity as I can a newly bought car; nor, at life's end, will I measure my contribution to creating a civilization of love as I might measure my bank account's increase. Great vision, purpose, and values are transcendent, intangible, and spiritual. And, ultimately, we will find the courage and will to pursue these spiritual ends authentically only when we, too, are spiritual—that is, when we feel connected to others and to our world in some real and not theoretical way, when we believe that there is more to the human person than can be seen, when we sense ourselves called to higher purpose, when we experience ourselves in communion with some power greater than ourselves, and when we become convinced that there is indeed bigger meaning to this world—and that we are part of that bigger meaning.

The path to courage, to the heart of any great strategy, ends with a conclusion that I do not doubt but cannot prove: if you don't have a spirituality, you won't find the interior means to remain committed in some deep-in-the-bones way to any transcendent purpose.

To be holy or to repair the world or to build a civilization of love are just words on a page, even trite clichés to some people. For others, they are a reason to live and to struggle, a path to peace and meaning. What turns mere words into great purpose? Take it personally. Get over yourself. Go to the God of your life and ask "in the way one friend speaks to another . . . now telling one's concerns and asking counsel about them" (#54).

I know that you are hot and tired, but keep going. If you are looking for God, God will find you.

How or where do you find the courage to persevere with difficult challenges or toward ambitious goals?

"Be bold, and mighty forces will come to your aid": how do you react to that statement and how do you understand it?

Create New Strategy for a New Time

Navigate a complex and fast-changing world.

Create strategy for your whole life.

Discover Your Mighty Purpose

Evaluate the world you've inherited.

Envision the future worth fighting for.

Articulate a purpose worth living for.

Embrace values worth standing for.

Put heart into strategy to give it life.

PART THREE

Choose Wisely

Learn to use your head and your heart.

Listen to the still, small voice.

Make Every Day Matter

Get the mind-set for getting results.

*Use a spiritual technology for
purposeful living.*

8

Make Great Choices
Learn to Use Your Head and Your Heart

L eaders build a solid foundation: they know their purpose, have an ambitious vision of the future, and stand for values that are not for sale.

It's essential that this core foundation endure through time, because little else around us will. Every effective person, family, or organization eventually learns the lesson that follows: create an enduring core, but be prepared to change everything else.

Two Stanford professors uncovered that very same lesson while researching the attributes that distinguish great companies from mediocre ones. The best companies have nonnegotiables at their core, some set of values or a mission that they won't sacrifice or compromise. Yet, at the same time, these companies evolve and grow—constantly. Recall the story of a J. P. Morgan that refurbished its business lines almost continuously. At our best, we combined an unchanging Morgan way of business and a relentless drive to improve by innovating and responding to changing business conditions. Or, as those Stanford researchers put it in their best-selling *Built to Last*: "preserve the core and stimulate progress."[1]

They were preaching a sermon that equally applies to the business of our lives: identify your core nonnegotiables, and then cultivate the strategic freedom to change everything else as circumstances require. If you have no core principles, you will fail. If you can't engage a changing world, you will fail. Winning companies and individuals learn to do both well.

And so this book now shifts focus, from building an enduring foundation to the challenge of making good decisions in a rapidly changing world. While the previous chapters have invited us to articulate some abiding purpose and vision to tide us through the dozen jobs we may hold in a lifetime, the coming chapters focus on how we can make better decisions when choosing those dozen different jobs, or deciding to marry, or forming our lifestyle, or facing other dilemmas.

Countless self-help guides promise to coach us through such decisions but at the cost of slicing our lives into pieces. That is, we end up buying one book for help with career choices and another for relationship decisions. Those books each help us through one kind of choice but don't equip us with a general skill set relevant for all kinds of choices—which is exactly what we need: a set of decision-making tools and skills that serve us regardless of the dilemma we have to resolve. So, instead of looking outside ourselves for answers in bookstore shelves when we face major decisions, we will learn to look inside ourselves with ever-greater confidence.

By making good choices, we will better embody Cardinal Newman's wise maxim: "To live is to change, and to be perfect is to have changed often."[2]

Consider the endless succession of choices that fill a lifetime:

- I'm graduating from college: should I find an accounting job, go to law school, or do volunteer work for a year?

- I'm forty; my job pays well but bores me; my career may have peaked and leveled out: Should I move on or stay put? Should I consider less remunerative but more fulfilling work?

- I've started discussing marriage with someone I'm dating. I had imagined "knowing the one," but real-life decisions aren't as clear as fairy-tale ones.

- I'm president of XYZ Corp. and considering a merger that would greatly boost earnings but entail substantial layoffs. I've made tough business decisions but am having trouble deciding whether to do this deal.

- I spent the past thirty years wishing I could play more golf; now I'm retired and am terrified that golf is the only thing I have to do. How do I make the most of my remaining productive life?

Millions of Americans confront these dilemmas right now, and every one of us regularly grapples with similar choices. Today's young adults will likely slalom through a half-dozen or more job choices in a lifetime, and meanwhile make decisions about relationships, finances, retirement, housing, and God knows what else. No one thrives in the developed world without learning to operate a computer or an ATM; neither will one thrive without a sound technology for making personal choices.[3]

Yet we are, by some measures, dreadfully inept decision makers. For example, it's reported that in any given year, more than 20 percent of us are looking to change jobs. Sometimes that's because our careers have reached a plateau or because market conditions force us to flee a declining industry. But many people are simply realizing that they stumbled into a job or career path that never really suited their gifts or temperament in the first place. We aren't any more effective when it comes to our most consequential relationship decisions: nearly half of U.S. marriages end in divorce. Corporate mergers fare even worse than marital ones: merger deals "fail to produce desired results almost 75 percent of the time," according to Harvard Business School's *Decision Making*.[4]

We know that bad outcomes don't always indicate bad decisions. Good marriages require lifelong work, sacrifice, compromise, and mutual support. Marriages fall apart for all kinds of reasons, sometimes not because the decision to wed was misguided but because either partner or both stopped working at the marriage. The partners may have chosen well (this chapter's concern) but failed to live out their choice day by day (a following chapter's concern).

Of course, not every sort of decision frustrates us. We probably confront more decisions in a week than our ancestors faced in a year, and we make most of them well. We choose between competing cell-phone providers, decide whether to buy our favorite peanut butter or the brand on sale, and figure out what to do with our free time. Ask me which of two mortgage loan proposals is cheapest, and I'll give you a definitive answer if a pocket calculator is handy.

But we can't resolve most of our consequential life decisions by punching numbers into calculators. The straightforward choice between two mortgage proposals may follow a gut-wrenching decision to accept a job transfer and relocate my family. I agonize over my spouse's career, my own job alternatives if I refuse the transfer, the impact on my young children, and whether I want to live far away from relatives and friends.

We can't easily manage the dizzying mental spiral of facts, values, and desires that figure into the decision. So we end up choosing by the seat of our pants, or we succumb to pressure from outsiders with agendas. We may compartmentalize by focusing only on our job prospects, as if our work life won't affect our family life. Some of us pay too much attention to feelings and thus make irrational, emotionally driven decisions. Others of us feel comfortable only with tangibles we can measure or count, so we completely ignore our inner voice (later we'll discuss just what that inner voice might mean and whether we can rely on it).

What we need is a rigorous method for decision making that incorporates both hard facts and intangibles such as feelings, values, and religious beliefs. Instead of compartmentalizing, we need to make whole-life decisions for whole-life strategies.

We need to choose wisely. That means using our heads to assess our talents, circumstances, opportunities, and beliefs; and it means using our heart and spirit to make free choices that bring peace rather than regrets.

The X Factor

Bringing our heart and spirit into the middle of major life choices may sound a bit like relying on a Ouija board, but researchers have long known that decision making is an art, not a sterile science of lining up a few facts. Even in the hardheaded, bottom-line business world, the Harvard Business Essentials guide *Decision Making* tells us that "research indicates that 45% of executives rely on their intuition rather than on facts in running their businesses."[5]

Some of those executives are making awful decisions, but others make winning choices by drawing on a skill that Alden Hayashi once described in the *Harvard Business Review*: "The consensus is that the higher up on the corporate ladder people climb, the more they'll need well-honed business instincts. In other words, intuition is one of the X factors that separate the men from the boys."[6] Take, for example, the McDonald's chief executive who successfully turned around the restaurant chain's performance. When the *Wall Street Journal* asked what methodology the company used to scan its vast ranks of rising managers and pick the emerging leaders, the chief executive said that "some of it is structural," through training programs and screening tools, but "some of it is by gut."[7]

But here's the problem. We know that good judgment is crucial to business, relationship, and career decisions. But we don't understand how good judgment works and why some people have it and others don't—why some people, for example, choose suitable marriage partners while others reel from one disastrous relationship to another. We can't even name the skill we're talking about: Hayashi's article calls it the "X factor" and a chief executive at a sophisticated multinational company calls it "gut." In short, we don't really understand this skill, can't name it, don't know how to acquire it, and, as a result, don't really know how valuable it is.

Yet the difference between happiness and misery often lies in the ability to choose well, whether pondering jobs or marriage partners, resolving ethical dilemmas, or deciding whether to speak or keep one's mouth shut in a sensitive moment. Our ancestors seemed to have understood better the profound difference good judgment can make across a lifetime; consequently, they cherished wisdom more deeply than our culture does today. Consider this eloquent passage from the Old Testament book of Proverbs:

> Happy are those who find wisdom,
>   and those who get understanding,
> for her income is better than silver,
>   and her revenue better than gold.
> She is more precious than jewels,
>   and nothing you desire can compare with her.
> . . .
> She is a tree of life to those who lay hold of her;
>   those who hold her fast are called happy.
> The Lord by wisdom founded the earth;
>   by understanding he established the heavens.
> (Proverbs 3:13–15, 18–19)

The passage points to an unfortunate irony of our era; its author exclaims that wisdom and understanding are more precious than silver, gold, or jewels. Our present-day culture by and large champions the opposite mind-set: I could care less about wisdom as long as I can get my hands on the gold and silver! Yet we know where that attitude has gotten us: the furious pursuit of money, things, fame, and power has made many folks wealthier but apparently no happier or wiser than their grandparents of more modest means.

The root of the word *wisdom* means "seeing" or "knowing." The imagery is apt. Modern culture's self-absorbed pursuit of wealth and fame as life's be all and end all is both shortsighted and ignorant. We don't see that we are on the wrong track. We don't know that the money and things our culture prods us to chase won't provide the deep meaning and purpose we crave as humans. We lack wisdom.

But we can acquire wisdom. The real marvel of the Proverbs passage is the claim that we mere humans can manifest the same awesome wisdom and understanding by which the Lord founded the earth and established the heavens. Wisdom is not a mysterious X factor that some are born with and others will forever lack. Rather, each of us can become wiser than we are today. To be sure, wisdom will remain to some extent both a gift and a mystery; there may be near-foolproof recipes for pancakes, but there is no assured path to infallibly wise choices. As an ancient wise man of Israel bluntly put it, "Wisdom is at home in the mind of one who has understanding, but it is not known in the heart of fools" (Proverbs 14:33). The first step toward attaining wisdom is to desire it in the heart.

The fool doesn't even desire wisdom because he doesn't recognize its value. The fool sees only the value of the next rung on the corporate ladder, an even bigger house, a third car, an attractive spouse, appearing on television, or being the richest person in the neighborhood. But the fool doesn't perceive that wisdom is more precious than any of these human fancies. We take our first step along the path to wisdom simply by wanting it.

As with anything else we want, we then figure out how to get it. The title of the seventeenth-century Spanish Jesuit Baltasar de Gracián's book, The Art of Worldly Wisdom, is instructive. The wisdom we seek is neither an exact science nor a vague gut feeling but an art. And as with most arts, we pursue it by learning certain practices and applying them consistently and patiently; we improve with time and practice.

We also see in Gracián's title that the wisdom we seek is spiritually grounded, but it is also worldly. Wisdom makes us whole people who are spiritual yet fully immersed in the world. Because we've lost sight of wisdom's worldly characteristics, we seldom even use the word nowadays—I can't remember hearing wisdom in the seventeen years I worked in the intellectually demanding business of investment banking. We stereotypically associate wisdom with ethereal, philosophical musings that dawn on us as we look back over a lifetime from the perch of old age. Wisdom may be nice to come by and comforting in old age but largely irrelevant to the day-to-day business of living. As we interview prospective hires for our companies, we seldom ask ourselves, Will this person be able to make wise choices? Rather, we worry about the candidate's technical skills because we want to remove the emotional, unreliable human factor in favor of objective, numbers-driven decision making. But judging by our dismal track records, we ought to realize by now that our obsession with the numbers and the measurables sometimes provides nothing more than highly sophisticated analysis as a rationale for fundamentally dumb choices!

So we need to put the human factor back into decision making by cultivating an art of worldly wisdom. When the Jesuit Gracián conceived that title, he was taking a cue from his spiritual father, Ignatius of Loyola, whose own insights into good judgment will guide the art of wisdom highlighted in the pages to come. Ignatius's insights ring true today, some five centuries after he penned them, because they sprang from real, often painful life experience. Loyola didn't sit in an ivory tower and map out decision trees, what-if analyses, and other decision technologies (helpful as those are). Rather, he refined his decision-making approach in part by working through the same dilemmas that vex all of us; after all, who hasn't suffered one or more of the following:

- My heart was set on a career path when a bitter setback dashed my plans. (Recall Ignatius the would-be soldier and courtier whose military career was shattered by the same cannonball that damaged his leg.)

- I have a vague dream of what I want to accomplish in life but not a clear plan for achieving it. I have deep spiritual beliefs, but I can't figure out how to connect them to a real-world occupation. (Recall Ignatius, after his conversion, imbued with a fervent desire to imitate the greatest saints in serving God but unable to translate that dream into a viable life plan.)

- I know I can make some difference in the world, but I lack confidence because of my meager natural gifts; I don't look the part for success in the modern world. (Think of Ignatius at the University of Paris: short, balding, limping, far older than his classmates, and hardly the most accomplished or smartest in class.)

• My circumstances keep changing, for better or for worse, and I find that I must keep adapting my life plans in response. (Remember Ignatius, expelled from the Holy Land, and suddenly forced to make a new life plan. Later, he arrived in Paris and serendipitously encountered a handful of fabulously talented and like-minded fellow students: he and they had to figure out how to turn this happy circumstance into concrete opportunity.)

Ignatius hit dead ends, made mistakes, was surprised by circumstances, and sometimes didn't know what to do. Sound familiar? Those sometimes-searing experiences were grist for his own personal decisions. But more crucially, once combined with divine grace, his experiences and reflection yielded a decision-making methodology that is core to the *Spiritual Exercises*. Some of its practices echo what wisdom traditions have emphasized for centuries; other ideas, radical in their time, have since been validated by modern research; still other practices remain Ignatius's proprietary insights into good decision making. We tap his exercises (and supplement them with some modern best practices) to highlight seven skills and attitudes that will make us wiser people who can bring head, heart, and spirit together to make high-quality decisions:

• Take charge of your life.
• Retreat to go forward.
• Control the controllables.
• Free yourself.
• Recognize consolation and desolation.
• Get a (real) friend.
• Do it over again . . . and again.

Take Charge of Your Life—through a Hopeful, Proactive, World-Open Attitude

The best decision makers have often figured out the answer before anyone asks them the question. That is, because they've done the foundational work of the previous chapters, they easily tackle decisions that bewilder the unprepared. Recall, for example, how Johnson & Johnson executives decided on a nationwide Tylenol recall without even assessing the financial costs or public-relations consequences. They weren't reckless; rather, they valued their company's integrity and intuitively grasped, as Dave Collins put it, that "there really was no choice" but to recall Tylenol.

Individuals are often stuck in the opposite predicament when major choices arise. They don't really know who they are, what they stand for, or where they are heading. Their deliberations therefore dissolve into a stressful, haphazard free-for-all because they cannot weigh the relevant trade-offs. The right choice between two job opportunities—one better paying and the other more fulfilling—may largely rest on one's purpose and values, and the middle of a decision is hardly the right moment to figure out what those purposes and values are.

But there's more to good choices than purpose and values. Good life choices also involve our circumstances, interests, talents, and resources—things that vary from person to person and that change often in life. For instance, Nanette Schorr wouldn't be able to do her current job in legal services if she hadn't passed the bar exam, learned to negotiate, or been able to write legal briefs, any more than I could become a professional baseball pitcher throwing seventy-mile-per-hour fastballs in a ninety-five-mile-per-hour profession.

We instill appropriate ambition and optimism when we remind young children that anyone can grow up to be president or encourage college students to follow their bliss in choosing careers. But we also need to instill a strategic approach toward life. Recall that strategy is not only about the ends we seek but also about the means to get there. My deep desire to be president (or a teacher, lawyer, or baseball player) needs to be coupled with a frank inventory of whether I really want it badly (my interests), have the necessary skills (my talents), can find the money and other support to make it happen (resources), and can freely commit myself to following my dream (circumstances). What's more, each person's talents, interests, resources, and circumstances differ, and each person's situation changes over time. The single person can freely pursue alternatives that the father of four cannot; and the father can pursue different alternatives after those children are raised and educated. Key to good choices, then, is the preparation done beforehand: the foundational sense of purpose and values, and an up-to-date inventory of our current interests and circumstances. With that self-inventory in hand, we're prepared to make tough choices, and sometimes our self-inventory can even make tough choices seem easy.

A single friend of mine—I'll call her Martha—decided to adopt a newborn child. The decision transformed her finances, free time, lifestyle, the kinds of jobs she could pursue, and countless other things. When I asked about her decision process, Martha said, "A friend asked, in the course of conversation, whether I'd ever thought of adopting, and I thought, Hey, *that's a great idea*, and almost right away started looking into it."

That's it? One of the smartest women I know had blithely embarked on a momentous life choice as the result of a friend's casual comment? Well, the adoption process was complicated, of course, so Martha's initial resolve was tested and confirmed by the sheer passage of time, the legal hurdles she had to clear, crises along the way, and the mounting expense of the process.

But as I reflected further, it became clear that the decision seemed to come easily only because Martha had long prepared for it. She knew her interests and circumstances. Her desire to care for a child hadn't just popped into her head one morning. "I've always loved kids, and if life had been different I'd have ended up with more than this one [her adopted child]." She had long been involved in charities that educated young children.

Of course, child rearing isn't merely a matter of desire; circumstances and resources come into play, and Martha judged that her work obligations wouldn't infringe on the attention she would need to devote to a child. What's more, she understood her financial circumstances well and had managed her money carefully enough throughout her working life to assume financial responsibility for a child.

Her conversation with a friend had crystallized into concrete opportunity a desire that had long percolated. As she put it, "I was probably mentally prepared. . . . I do believe that a lot of the 'work' of making the decision had been done subconsciously." If she had not understood her circumstances and resources well, she easily could have blundered.

If Dave Collins and Nanette Schorr teach us to prepare for life's major decisions by knowing enduring purpose and values, Martha's example shows that we also need to track our ever-changing circumstances, talents, interests, and resources. All come into play in major choices, and by understanding them in advance, we navigate choices more confidently.

Still, it's not just knowing one's purpose and talents but manifesting a world-loving, open attitude to living that purpose and using those talents. Consider the Gospel parable (Matthew 25:14–30) about servants who are entrusted with "talents"—a certain amount of money—during their master's journey. One of them, fearful of losing what was provided him, buries his one talent in the ground and is later upbraided as wicked and slothful for not investing productively. In contrast, the good and faithful servant pleases his master by investing his five talents to earn five more.

Jesus wasn't offering investment advice; he was illustrating two attitudes toward the world and one's giftedness. The wicked servant hunkers down fearfully; in a world where choices can go wrong, he shrinks from making any choice at all. But when we refrain from making a choice about how to use our talents, we make a momentous choice—by not developing and using our talent, we choose to waste it. The good servant, conversely, sees a world of possibilities and so acts out of a hopeful and world-loving attitude. He makes much of his talents by using them fully.

My friend Martha didn't know she would end up adopting a child as she saved money during her early working years, but by saving she was creating tomorrow's opportunities. When a conversation opened an opportunity for Martha, she seized it. Instead of waiting for life to happen to her, she drew on her resources, imagination, and determination to create an opportunity to nurture a child.

Many of us may lack financial resources, but we do have more than we imagine: intellect, time, education, friends, a family, proximity to those in need, and so on. I know the retired president of a hospital system who no longer pulls the levers of power he did as a well-known executive. But he now relishes his time (a "talent" he previously lacked) to pursue small random acts of kindness, like pausing during early morning winter walks to transfer neighbors' just-delivered newspapers from the curbside to their front stoops.

We all have more talents than we dream of, and more opportunities to use them than we typically consider. Just compare our lives to those of Jesus' listeners. A talent was a considerable sum of money in Jesus' day, and few of his listeners could have aspired to acquire so much during short, hardscrabble lifetimes that often ended before a fortieth birthday. Now we live in a world transformed and possess talents unimaginable to Jesus' contemporaries. We live prosperously in safer, comfortable dwellings furnished with productivity-enhancing technology. Libraries, televisions, and computers place centuries of accumulated wisdom at our fingertips. We generally live decades longer than our ancestors did. Thanks to insurance, social security systems, and medical advances, we can be more productive and secure in our older age. What will we do to keep developing and using the health, knowledge, longevity, social networks, time, and savings, among countless other resources that we have (and Jesus' listeners lacked)? Will we, like the wicked servant, bury these talents, or will we invest them as productively as the good and faithful servant?

Whatever our talents, the tried but true saying applies: "Your talent is God's gift to you; what you do with it is your gift to God." That is a deeply strategic invitation to take stock of our many gifts and talents, relish them, develop them, and find ways to deploy them throughout life's changing circumstances. That's not only our gift to God but a gift to ourselves as well, because, as the late psychologist Abraham Maslow put it, "If you set out to be less than you're capable of, you won't be happy."

The least successful life strategists wait passively for things to happen; the most successful ones make things happen. The former let chance events steer their future; the latter drive their destiny and shape the future.

What are ten talents—resources, opportunities, networks, gifts, and abilities—that you seldom think about?

Which talents are you using well? Which ones have you not been using?

In what ways are you passive about your life? How do you manifest the hopeful, open attitude to grasp whatever opportunities may come?

Retreat to Go Forward—
by Learning to Reflect

The perennial all-star baseball pitcher Tom Glavine once had to decide whether to remain with the illustrious, world-beloved New York Mets or abandon them for a job offer from the team nearer his family home, the dread Atlanta Braves (not that I have a point of view). A journalist covering Glavine's choice noted that whenever Glavine pitches, "he must make hundreds of decisions every time he takes the mound, many in a split second." But while choosing whether to remain in New York or relocate to Atlanta, "Glavine used every second of the six weeks he allotted himself to make a decision."[8]

So what? Everyone knows that deciding to throw a curveball differs from deciding to relocate one's family. But Glavine's story reinforces the simple but often overlooked insight that we need different decision-making attitudes for different sorts of decisions. Sometimes the right choice will be intuitively clear (as when Glavine picks pitches), but other sorts of choices (about job changes, careers, and marriage partners, for example) will require considerable reflection.

In his best seller *Blink*, Malcolm Gladwell profiled professionals who make high-quality judgments in, well, the blink of an eye.[9] Battlefield commanders, for example, often piece together scattered bits of conflicting information to make uncannily sound, split-second tactical judgments. Likewise, baseball pitchers like Glavine learn to make good choices within very short time frames.

But our time-pressed culture, obsessed with instant gratification, is forcing us to blink our way through decisions that could benefit from a longer gaze. We barge through doubts rather than explore them. We construe second thoughts as weakness rather than potential wisdom. Many working environments prize extreme decisiveness. A colleague of mine used to describe one macho senior manager like this: "If he hasn't had the chance to make a couple of major, on-the-spot decisions by lunchtime, he doesn't feel like he's having a good day."

But savvy decision makers know that not all choices can be made on the fly. I worked alongside foreign-exchange and bond traders who made split-second decisions for a living, yet they recognized that some decisions required a very different approach. They periodically withdrew from the market pandemonium to take stock of the world beyond their trading floor, to examine whether they were fully using their strengths, to determine whether they were missing new business opportunities, and to explore new strategic directions.

Corporate conference centers cater to management groups looking to escape the distractions and bustle of everyday business to conduct what's often called a "strategic retreat." These gunslingers-on-retreat are unknowingly heeding the wisdom of Ignatius Loyola, who recommended "withdrawing from all friends and acquaintances, and from all earthly concerns; for example, by moving out of one's place of residence and taking a different house or room where one can live in the greatest possible solitude" (#20).

Ironically, these bottom-line-oriented companies have assimilated a practice that the spiritually minded have pretty much forsaken. Once upon a time, religious believers also undertook annual retreats (it was a thriving practice long before corporations caught on to the idea or adopted the word). Today, corporate retreat centers flourish while the practice of personal spiritual retreats, after falling to near desuetude, is only slowly regaining momentum.

Simply put, sometimes we need to retreat in order to go forward, and our blink culture may have blinded us to that fact. We may be able to track down acquaintances instantaneously with a cell phone, but we can't so easily dial up feelings, thoughts, and emotions that bubble into full consciousness only with time and close attention. Yes, we can effortlessly turn up countless job openings on an employment search Web site, but no search engine can sort through our needs, interests, and desires. We will benefit from managing the business of our lives the same way savvy management teams deal with their affairs: by retreating on a regular basis—whether or not a major life decision looms—to remind ourselves of our purpose, vision, talents, and circumstances.

At a minimum, we'll find sufficient quiet to hear our own thoughts, the perspective to look beyond daily life's chaos, and the opportunity to focus on long-term concerns rather than short-term crises. But spiritual people tap into other vital benefits during these moments as well: the perspective that the world is bigger than our own self-interest, and the consoling awareness that we are not alone in the universe.

Control the Controllables—by Focusing Your Energy Where It Counts

My friend Martha created through adoption an opportunity to nurture a child. We control the controllables whenever we discover opportunities to express our purpose and vision in our real-life circumstances.

Many other people might love to adopt but lack the financial resources to support a child, and so we also control the controllables when we peaceably understand (and accept) what we cannot do, manage, change, or control.

Healthy individuals know the difference. They focus energy and effort where they can exert influence and control, and they don't obsess over what lies beyond their control. That mind-set preserves mental health, but it's also a graceful, and grace-filled, acceptance that the world is not about us. This is not our world, but God's, and much of it—indeed, much that affects us—lies outside our control.

The Jesuit Walter Ciszek's life (1904–1983) embodied this wisdom. When I was a Jesuit seminarian, Fr. Ciszek and I dined for a while in the same large Jesuit community. This quiet, self-effacing old man stood about as high as my chest and seemed unremarkable by any conventional measure. Many of us regularly bypassed his company at dinner for that of more entertaining, livelier colleagues.

Now I laugh to myself about it. Fr. Ciszek's cause for sainthood is wending its way through the tortuous Vatican machinery. I may someday have to explain to friends that I lived with a saint and paid scant attention to him. I suspect that this says something encouraging about the self-effacing nature of true saints and something discouraging about me!

Even though we lavished little attention on Fr. Ciszek, we all knew his remarkable life story, chronicled in <u>He Leadeth Me</u> and <u>With God in Russia.</u> Sent to Russia as a young priest, Ciszek was accused during World War II of being a Vatican spy and was shuttled around Soviet gulags and remote work camps for two decades. Ciszek passed days in a tiny cell that was "about seven by twelve feet, with grimy stone walls and one little window high in the wall. The room was always dark." But that wasn't the bad part: that seven-by-twelve cell was home to as many as a dozen people: "At night, we all huddled together on the rough-hewn benches to sleep. If someone turned over in his sleep, he was liable to wake the whole crowd." [10]

Imagine days with nothing to look forward to beside the next interrogation or the next meager meal. Compounding the physical privations was the frustration that things weren't working out according to Ciszek's plans. He went to Russia to do things; how endlessly demoralizing to sit in a prison and chew over the bitter reality that he was doing nothing, day after day.

That is, Ciszek relates, until a personal epiphany dawned. "God's will was not hidden somewhere 'out there' . . . the situations [in which I found myself] were his will for me. What he wanted was for me to accept these situations as from his hands, to let go of the reins and place myself entirely at his disposal." [11] Ciszek's options were to lament endlessly what he couldn't control or to fulfill his purpose in the small corner of the world he could control, his cell.

Fr. Ciszek in his jail cell or work camp, praying and occasionally interacting with jailers or fellow prisoners, is a poignant embodiment of a well-known phrase in Jesuit life: *age quod agis*—"do what you're doing!" We tend to obsess over what we wish we were doing, or what we might be doing instead of our boring jobs, or what we would like to be doing that someone else is doing, or what we could have been doing if our luck had been better. Such preoccupations distract us from whatever real opportunity lies right in front of us. If we do what we are doing, we focus on the opportunity at hand, even (or perhaps especially) if all we can do is sit in a jail cell, pray, think good thoughts, and treat our captors with civility and kindness.

None of us finds peace or performs effectively without learning Fr. Ciszek's hard-won lesson, because each successive phase of life brings new circumstances that change what is and isn't within our control. While we are young, we may have energy, time, and freedom but modest financial resources. In middle age, we may have young families to raise and love but limited freedom to take on other obligations and opportunities. Retirement often bestows the talent of time once more. Our challenge, like Fr. Ciszek's, is to accept peaceably what we cannot control and make the most of what lies within our control, never losing sight of our purpose and vision along the way.

At life's end, only one choice may lie within our control: whether to die with dignity. My father was only fifty-five when an unexpected cancer diagnosis precipitated a nine-month slide to death. A man who had emigrated from an impoverished island to make a better life for himself and who had always worked and successfully supported a family, suddenly found himself relying on that family to bathe, shave, and feed him. His last great strategic choice: to die with dignity or to become a knot of resentment against the unfairness of it all. He chose well.

My father never heard the phrase "control the controllables," though he intuitively grasped it. That's likewise true for Fr. Ciszek and his Jesuit forbears. This principle's essence seems embedded in their style of working and in their spirituality.

Consider a gung-ho sixteenth-century Jesuit in Asia who was caught by a sudden squall while piloting his tiny boat from one remote mission outpost to another. He shouted to his frightened young Jesuit colleague at the oars, "Pray to God, sailor, but row for shore." He was echoing a saying famously attributed to Ignatius himself: "Work as if all depended on you; trust as if all depended on God."[12] Ignatius's successor as general of the Jesuits, Diego Lainez, put it more bluntly: "While it is true that God could speak by the mouth of an ass, this would be considered a miracle. We are tempting God when we expect miracles. This would certainly be the case in a man who lacks common sense but who hopes to be a success merely by praying for it."[13]

When controlling the controllables, be resourceful and do everything in your power to take charge of your life. At the same time, humbly and gracefully accept that it is God's world. The self-centered arrogantly presume to control everything around them, even the humans unfortunate enough to interact with them at work or home. But the wise live the insight of the Serenity Prayer often associated with Alcoholics Anonymous: "Lord, give me the courage to change the things I can, the serenity to accept what I cannot change, and the wisdom to know the difference."[14]

Serenity is essential, for example, when we must hang on to an unfulfilling, demanding job because it's the only viable source of health-care benefits and financial support for our family. But courage is essential if we have alternatives either to enhance our job or to leave it entirely. Sometimes bold initiative is possible and imperative; at other times, the best (and only) strategic choice is to make the most of the opportunity at hand. Give us the wisdom, Lord, to know whether serenity or courage (usually it's both) is required.

We need similar wisdom when it comes to our personal circumstances. For example, we cannot venture back in time to undo some injustice inflicted by an unfaithful spouse or an unscrupulous manager. Our only way to assert control may be to let go of the long-nursed anger and pain that remains from such unhappy episodes. Or, no matter how deeply I love my substance-abusing adult child, I can do only so much to pull him or her from that hell. The courageous do everything within their control but wisely and serenely accept what they cannot change; the rest of us drive ourselves to distraction trying to bend the world to our will, as if we might stand at the seashore and hold back the tide. Give us such wisdom, Lord.

Of course, even the saintly Fr. Ciszek needed time (and solitary confinement!) to achieve his equanimity, so the same virtue will likely develop in our own frenetic lives only through time and practice.

How can you retreat to go forward? What would it require in terms of time, schedule, and resources to reflect on your life? Who could help you arrange this?

How do you react to factors that are outside your control? What, or who, can help you figure out when it's time for acceptance and serenity, or for change and courage?

Free Yourself—
by Developing the Ability to Detach

Whenever we approach a major decision, Ignatius urges us to be "indifferent, that is, without any disordered affection" (#179). An anecdote or two will explain what he means and why indifference and disordered affection are supremely relevant concepts for all kinds of decisions.

A business reporter once delved into the curious phenomenon that many corporate merger deals never pay off for shareholders. One day we see two smiling chief executives shaking hands at the merger announcement; a few years later they are shaking their heads and investors are shaking their fists because yet another high-profile deal has flopped. The merger may have made plenty of headlines, but in retrospect, it didn't make a whole lot of financial sense.

The business reporter wondered why such flops happen. After all, the planet's brightest and best-paid lawyers, bankers, and corporate chieftains labor over these deals. How could they get it so wrong so often? The reporter questioned economists and business school professors, and surprisingly, heard the sort of answers that Ignatius of Loyola might offer: <u>many ill-conceived deals can be attributed to greed, pride, or ego.</u>

The people interviewed pointed out that chief executives sometimes receive hefty financial bonuses for completing a major deal, so greed might subtly cloud an executive's judgment as he or she considers whether to go forward with a proposed deal. Others speculated that even though some chief executives know that a large proportion of deals never pan out, they are nonetheless supremely confident that their deal will be the exception—pride deludes them into imagining that they can implement a complicated merger far more capably than their peers can. Ego enhancement is pride's cousin, and other economists theorized that some chief executives are beguiled into deals simply because it feels swell to see your picture in the papers after pulling off a huge transaction.

To be sure, no chief executive is consciously choosing to broker foolish deals in order to see his or her name in the papers or to collect a big bonus (well, virtually no chief executive). Rather, greed and pride infect us far more subtly. Ignatius of Loyola compared greed, pride, and similarly debilitating vices to false lovers—adulterers—who want to remain undetected. Just as an adulterer will be most successful when slinking around undiscovered, pride most insidiously affects our behavior when we're not fully aware that it's infiltrated our motivations. We feel as if we're objectively examining just the facts, but deep down we're predisposed to steer toward one outcome or another, like the chief executive who wants the big deal so badly that he blunders forward without adequately weighing the reasons to walk away.

The opposite also happens when we hang back from deciding to pursue a new direction or needed change because we're attached to the status quo. For example, we entrust senators and other elected leaders to formulate wise responses for the ever-evolving challenges facing our country, from new security threats to new technology-enabled opportunities. Yet even as new threats and opportunities emerge, elected officials sometimes cling to the same old solutions. Tom Daschle, the onetime Senate majority leader, lamented that

"the more time you spend here [in Washington and in the Senate],"
the more susceptible you are to "a mind-set that we did it this way
before, we should do it this way again."[15] Those senators, like chief
business executives, surely believe that they are objectively weighing the facts, but their judgment may be clouded by attachments
to their own status, their party, to fear of the unknown, or to fear
of associating their reputations with new ideas that might end up
failing.

Most of us worry about more mundane affairs than about merg-
ing companies or formulating national policy. We're deciding how
far away from home to let our daughter move for college, whether
it's time to buy a bigger house, or what to do about a troubled marriage. But our attachments—those false lovers—intrude on these
sorts of decisions as well. Just as greed- or pride-driven chief executives make unwise business choices, the same demons drive us to
buy houses or cars we can't afford, and thereby saddle ourselves
with ruinous debt.

Or, just like those senators, our attachments can hold us back
from making decisions and choices. George Simon, a leading family
therapist and author, explained in a conversation with me, "Often,
the biggest problem facing the couples I see is that they've become
'attached to their attachments'—something is not working, but
they are unwilling to make the changes and choices necessary to
better their lives and relationships."

Couples may engage George because of anger, unhappiness, and
pain in their marriage. They want him to make those symptoms go
away, but they themselves don't want to change the way they have
come to think about each other and relate to each other. It sometimes seems that they would prefer to keep complaining about the
situation rather than change it. They have become attached to the
state of affairs they have created. They're stuck. It may be unfulfilling, but it feels safer to them than risking the unknown.

George told me about Bob and Betty (needless to say, he zeal-
ously guarded their confidentiality by changing their names and
other details). Betty explained during their first session, "Bob isn't

pulling his weight at home. He doesn't listen, he forgets. When I need help managing the kids, he's watching television and drinking a beer, oblivious to it all." Bob more or less conceded to her version of events and said that Betty was "the perfect one," "the foundation" of their family. As the couple presented it, George's job was to help fix Bob; maybe he was depressed, for example, and needed medication?

But the story didn't quite compute. At work, Bob managed teams of accounting professionals, engaged sophisticated clients, and competently tracked copious financial details. George pointed out the enigma. "Could you two discuss something that's been puzzling me: Bob leaves home each morning and functions as a consummate professional; then he returns home and becomes a forgetful and sometimes recalcitrant child?"

George told me, "Couples sometimes drift into a situation where each starts to see the other, almost subconsciously, in a somewhat rigid role. Their relationship becomes inflexible, almost as if their family life is a play in which each person follows his or her script." He suspected that however Bob and Betty had first fallen into their patterns of thinking about and relating to each other, they had eventually become stuck in a loop. Betty derived satisfaction from being a competent household manager. Bob got used to not being depended on at home; that couldn't have felt good to him, so he slowly checked out and became less and less engaged in the family's affairs, and even started drinking a bit more. Once or twice he forgot her birthday, and those blows to Betty's sense of self-worth only drove her to cling more tightly to the household management, which salvaged some self-esteem. Betty saw herself as the organizer and Bob as undependable; Bob saw Betty as domineering and tuned her out. And so they spiraled into a less and less happy partnership.

But Bob and Betty were partners in holding themselves back from healthy change. They were digging themselves further and further into a groove. Ironically, their system worked (albeit dysfunctionally). Their roles complemented each other; they became attached to their unhealthy way of relating to each other.

But their roles were ultimately unfulfilling. Bob was frustrated at being marginalized in his own household, and when Betty spoke about the forgotten birthday, George saw that the so-called perfect one was, deep down, feeling lonely, depressed, and underappreciated. Both were unhappy, but both were conflict avoiders who feared taking the risk of throwing everything up in the air, confronting each other, and trading their now-familiar way of relating for unfamiliar new roles with each other.

So George rewrote their script; he asked Bob to manage the household every evening for a while. Two weeks later, an obviously unhappy couple showed up in his office. Bob had done an OK job, but Betty accused him of just putting on a show to impress the therapist; this angered Bob, who felt that his efforts were unappreciated.

A failed experiment? Not as George saw it: "My job was to help them figure out together how he could make her feel loved and she could make him feel needed," and by recasting their roles at home, "I was trying to jump-start them—against their inclinations—into relating to each other differently." In fact, as the session went on, Betty sheepishly admitted that Bob had worked hard to change and that she hadn't acknowledged the change appropriately. And instead of greeting that admission with a "whatever" shrug, Bob confessed that he understood her reluctance to trust him. But, he continued, "that change was tough for me; I need you to support me if I'm going to make this work over the long term." This wasn't their same old argument as if read from a script. They were slowly beginning to relate to each other in a different way, as peers and even as intimates, as three-dimensional people who each have lots of skills and lots of needs.

Some readers may wonder what Bob and Betty's story has to do with making major choices, the main topic of this chapter. After all, they weren't deciding whether to divorce, nor was this a morality tale of, say, a youth-obsessed Bob who chose an adulterous affair that destroyed his marriage.

But their story is very much about choice. It's as if, every day of their deteriorating relationship, Bob and Betty were asked, "Would you like a healthier, more energized, fulfilling relationship?" and, for a long time, they answered, "No thanks, we will choose to muddle through with our frustrating present one!"

The rest of us are susceptible to the same self-destructive (often hidden) choices whenever we're attached to some unhealthy perception of ourselves or our family, colleagues, and friends, or whenever we cling to our unfulfilling present rather than choose to take risks for a better future.

Imagine a parent who is asked, "Hey, would you like to help your adolescent become a healthy, independent adult by gradually giving her, in a responsible way, the increased independence she will need?" What loving parent would answer, "No thanks. I think I'll cling to my role as the obsessive caregiver because I still think of her as my little girl, and, besides, I've grown so attached to my fear of being an empty nester in ten years."

Or imagine a mature adult facing the question, Would you like to have a happy, trusting relationship again? Who would answer, "No, I think I will never trust again. I would prefer to forever remain bitter and nurse my resentment at being betrayed by a friend five years ago."

Which of us, asked if we wanted to rise to our fullest potential at work, would reply, "Nah. I'm so used to my lack of self-confidence that I'll keep choosing not to take the risk of speaking up in a meeting or applying for jobs that might better use my talents."

And, finally, what parents, asked whether they want to enable their children to have healthy adult relationships, would respond, "Not really. My husband and I really don't want to stop having the same old argument over and over again, even though it greatly increases the odds that our own children, when they themselves are adults, will end up adopting our dysfunctional pattern of relating."

Those embroiled right now in such cases (and thousands like them) don't perceive themselves as facing decisions: it's not like contemplating marriage, a job change, or a major purchase. But they confront an even more fundamental, all-encompassing decision: will you choose to pursue the best possible version of your life, business, and relationships, or will you settle for some deprived, energy-sapping, self-destructive life? The choice hinges on confronting and coming to grips with whatever unhealthy attachments might be holding us back.

The solution, as we stand before our lives, our loved ones, and every big professional or personal decision, is to shake free of attachments that might push us in the wrong direction or hold us back from heading in the right direction. Sometimes we're driven by the I-want-it-so-badly virus: I so wanted to get to the top of the company, or to attract that attractive person, or to be rich, or to be recognized as important, or to have the best house, or to have a more exciting life. In fact, we sometimes delude ourselves into thinking that the object of our affection (the job, the car, the partner, the house) must be right for us precisely because we want it so badly.

Sometimes our desires are in fact good indicators of where we need to go or what course we need to take (as the following pages will explore). But sometimes just the opposite is true. What I want so badly may scratch an ego itch but do nothing to further my purpose in life; it might even lead me astray of my purpose. Greed, pride, or a host of other debilitating drives can take powerful hold of us and are all the more pernicious because we're not fully aware of how deeply they may have affected our thinking. That's what Ignatius meant by an attachment to disordered affections that can undermine our judgment.

Or, as we see in Bob and Betty's case, sometimes we get attached to our attachments. We become used to the status quo, afraid of the unknown, desperate to avoid conflict, or unwilling to take a risk. In such cases, our attachments are not pushing us in the wrong direction; they are shackling us and holding us back. Thus, we shrink in front of choice and change. We lack the self-confidence to pursue the big promotion, the willingness to let our children grow into their own lives, or the openness to support our spouse as he or she grows in some new direction. In such cases, the I-want-it-so-badly virus shows up as "I wanted everything to stay as it was!"

Unfortunately, we can't count on having a George Simon to help us address what attachments might be clouding our judgment. We have to create our own moment of self-scrutiny during life and especially before major decisions. Pause, look within yourself, try to pinpoint all the motives at work, and drag them into the sanitizing light of day to sort out any unhealthy ones that might be pulling you toward bad decision making. By becoming aware of your inappropriate attachments, you greatly diminish their power to impair your reasoning. As Ignatius colorfully put it, our attachments can be like illicit lovers: they have power while they remain undetected, but once fully exposed, they often turn cowardly and vanish.

The goal is to reach the equilibrium that frees us to choose the healthiest path for our lives, our work, and our families. When a chief executive first sits down to consider that merger proposal, he or she needs to feel free to either consummate a deal or walk away at peace. The executive will do the right deal for good reasons but won't drift into doing a dumb deal for bad reasons. That's what Ignatius calls an attitude of indifference, and *indifference* is a tricky word that can cause confusion. He doesn't mean indifferent in the sense of not caring one way or the other, because we ought to care passionately about making sound career, marriage, money, and life-style choices. But precisely because we care so much, we need to approach each decision with the strategic freedom and openness to pursue whatever will be the best course of action.

A meditation in the Exercises illustrates the concept. Ignatius asks you to imagine that you have inherited a huge sum of money. What should you do with it? First make yourself free, Ignatius counsels, to pursue all appropriate strategic alternatives, "in such a way that there remains no inclination either to keep the acquired money or to dispose of it" (#155). Only then are you prepared to make a sound choice, guided by your sense of purpose and mission, and not swayed by some misguided attachment or short-sighted objective.

Read Consolation and Desolation—by Attending to Your Interior Signals

Javier Moso's story illustrates another of Ignatius's principles for choosing wisely: learn to read consolation and desolation.

Javier, named for the Jesuit cofounder Francis Xavier, lives in a part of the world where lots of people are named for Francis Xavier: Spain's Navarre province, where the saint's family castle still stands amid picturesque, rolling hills. After his father's death not many years ago, Javier, a lawyer, took leave from his legal practice to care for his mother, who was aging and ailing. It seems a stunning choice, given how contemporary culture so heavily associates status with career. "I'm a lawyer" sets more heads nodding at cocktail parties than, say, "I'm at home taking care of my mom." To our disgrace, it's become a joke in the business community that when a chief executive announces, "I'm resigning to spend more time with the family," we all think, *He's been fired and doesn't have another job yet.*

I wondered whether Javier felt uncomfortable at chance meetings with career-driven buddies or whether he resented the circumstances that forced him to change his life direction. He answered simply, "I'm happy doing what I'm doing; my mother is happy with me." He wasn't talking about superficial happiness but about a deeper, reassuring satisfaction that he's doing the right thing.

Javier might well be enjoying what Ignatius called "consolation." He associated consolation with one or more of the following: "courage and strength, consolations, tears, inspirations, and tranquility." Moreover, consolation often brings with it the inner confidence to follow through when one has chosen to pursue a difficult or unpopular (but worthy) path. Consolation, Ignatius says, "makes things easier and eliminates all obstacles, so that the persons may move forward in doing good" (#315).

Perhaps Javier feels happy because he's experiencing exactly that amalgam of feelings. Even though he is swimming against the cultural tide by giving up the income and status of his law practice, he feels as if he is swimming easily. He is aware of the trade-offs his choice entailed, yet those trade-offs don't weigh heavily on his heart. He feels not resentful but happy and peaceable.

Most everyone has experienced that same welcome feeling after anguishing over a painful choice to switch jobs, end a relationship, or accept a personal setback. At a certain moment, we stopped looking for ways to avoid our dilemma, tranquility descended, and we accepted what needed to be done. We moved forward with the same confidence and comfort that Javier felt. We might describe ourselves as finally being at peace with our decision. Ignatius would say that we might be enjoying consolation that confirms we are on the right path.

Most of us have also suffered the opposite feeling of lingering anguish and anxiety while contemplating a major choice. Ignatius calls that experience "desolation": "obtuseness of soul, turmoil within it, an impulsive motion toward low and earthly things, or disquiet from various agitations and temptations" (#317).

Our instinct is to do anything that might make such feelings go away. If I suffer disquiet from various agitations while pondering whether to break off a relationship, I just stop thinking about it. Or I rush ahead and break off the relationship to get the unpleasantness over with. Or I have a drink or two to anesthetize temporarily the disquiet that I'm feeling. None of these responses is the correct one when facing desolation.

Ignatius counsels just the opposite: to treat desolation as an internal early warning signal that something is not quite right with the way we are processing the decision, even though the brain may not yet have figured out exactly what or why. Desolation can indicate that we are about to choose unwisely or make an inappropriate commitment, so decision makers need to apply the brakes at the first whiff of desolation and scrutinize their thought process. Ignatius says, "During a time of desolation one should never make a change. Instead, one should remain firm and constant in the resolutions and in the decision which one had on the day before the desolation" (#318). In other words, don't barge ahead despite desolation; step back to devote further attention, thought, and meditation to the proposed decision.

By tracking patterns of consolation and desolation, we pick up vital clues that turn otherwise vague feelings into data that point the way toward good choices. Confusion, inner turmoil, discomfort, and anxiety all indicate desolation, and, if possible, we ought to probe further rather than make decisions while in its throes. Tranquility, confidence, hope, and inspiration all indicate consolation, a signal that our thinking may well be on the right path.

But Javier's consolation descended while he was already implementing his life choice, and what we're really after are tools to use while we're in the decision process. After all, we can't try out marriage for a few weeks and then decide to stick around or not depending on whether it feels consoling.

But we can take an imaginative dry run. Don't just fantasize about the honeymoon (we all like to do that); also imagine picking up the socks he refuses to put in the hamper, and nursing her through an illness, or struggling together with finances when he unexpectedly loses his high-status job, or sharing the sleep-deprived joy of raising children together. Pay careful attention to the feelings that percolate during the imaginative exercise, especially what might feel like consolation or desolation.

Then, imagine life without marrying the person, and likewise keep your emotional antennae well attuned to consolation or desolation. For example, you might consistently sense consolation's inner peace and confidence not only when imagining life together in richness and in health but equally when imagining unexpected illness or poverty. Ignatius would consider such consistent feelings of consolation a very powerful confirming signal that the person's thinking may be on the right track.

It can be difficult to even sense our inner motions, much less interpret them reliably. Some of us are so notoriously out of touch with our feelings that we realize only tomorrow that we feel sad about something today. I once heard someone, asked whether he had ever had an out-of-body experience, say, "Out-of-body experience? Heck, I'm working hard just to have an in-my-body experience!" That's another reason Ignatius counsels retreating-to-go-forward in a serene environment while pondering life changes: we can better tune in to consolations or desolations when we are removed from daily life's ambient noise. Still, no matter how clear the emotional signals may seem, Ignatius would counsel that pitfalls abound in the delicate art of deciphering them. Pocket calculators deliver the correct answer—first time, every time. But reading consolations and desolations is trickier, and the last thing he would suggest, with respect to marriage or any other major decision, is simply to rely on your inner voice alone. Good choices involve head, heart, and spirit, and the best indicator of a sound choice is that head, heart, and spirit converge around a common answer. That is, when a prospective decision seems rational and corresponds with one's sense of purpose and values, and engenders feelings of consolation, we're probably on the right track.

That convergence doesn't always happen. Lots of decisions are complicated. Rarely do our inner motions, logic, and values align completely. Often we're plagued by conflicting feelings: I might feel great peace while imagining raising a child with my potential spouse but great anxiety while imagining us aging together. Our head pulls one way and our heart seems to pull another.

Or, even worse, we mistake unhealthy attachments for consolation: I may be exhilarated when I imagine seducing a married woman or becoming wealthy through embezzlement or daydreaming about the prestige that would result from politically outmaneuvering colleagues for a major promotion. Ignatius warns never to mistake base satisfactions for proper consolation, which only draws us to worthy goals.

But even positive feelings toward worthy goals can lead us astray now and then. A good-hearted parent, priest, or office worker might consider new opportunities to serve and support family, parishioners, or colleagues. The priest may feel a burst of consolation when imagining how a program for young adults could serve a vital community need, and how he could economize for the parish by assuming some duties of a paid external accountant, and how an expanded program of worship services could benefit the parish's spiritual life. He interprets his enthusiasm for these worthy initiatives as a consoling signal to rush forward with all of them, only to find himself exhausted within six months, cranky toward his parishioners, and not managing to implement any of his plans well.

On the one hand, our inner voice is an invaluable source of data for high-quality choices. And Ignatius's spiritual technology of reading consolations and desolations is a powerful methodology for interpreting our inner voice. On the other hand, we have to use our heads as well as our hearts and keep our life compass attuned to our ultimate purpose as we do so. Because it can be so difficult to sort through conflicting thoughts and feelings, Ignatius advises us to find good company for this process.

Think of a major decision you will likely face within the next few years. What attachments could impair your ability to make a sound choice?

Can you recall a moment of consolation during a past decision-making process, for example, an inner peace that might have descended as you reached a tough choice, or a feeling of courage that you could carry through with the consequences of a difficult decision?

Think of an occasion on which some unhealthy attachment drove you to a dumb decision. How aware were you of your attachment during the decision process?

Get a Real Friend— by Finding Wise Associates

I was asked during my J. P. Morgan career to relocate from New York for a job in Japan. I thought it would be a fascinating cultural experience, the job would challenge me, and I would acquire skills that dovetailed with my long-term interests. For all these reasons, I leaned toward taking the job.

However, the administrative job waiting for me in Japan would have less cachet in our swaggering, macho industry than did the investment banker job I would surrender. And it was no small matter that, in an industry that is all about accumulating money, my long-term earnings trajectory could diminish—that is, I would no longer be on the fastest track to the heftiest bonuses.

I presented the trade-offs to a colleague and said I was leaning toward taking the job in Japan. Without hesitation, he said, "Why the . . . would you do that?" He knew the right answer— but for his life. Unfortunately, his advice so heavily reflected his own priorities—maximizing his earnings—that it left my priorities unconsidered. He was a great friend (and a great investment banker) but a lousy mentor when it came to helping me make a major decision.

Contrast him with another friend I've sometimes consulted about looming choices. He invariably responds to my quandaries of "on the one hand and on the other hand" with a simple question: "Well, which choice do you think will make you happier?" He doesn't mean ice-cream cone happy but that deeper happiness— consolation—that Javier Moso has found in caring for his aging mother.

My friend's style fits Ignatius of Loyola's description of the ideal spiritual coach, who "should not urge . . . to one state or manner of living more than to another. . . . [and therefore] ought not to lean or incline in either direction but rather . . . stand by like the pointer of a scale in equilibrium" (#15).

Good coaches for decision making don't interject their priorities and feelings but help you to unravel yours. We've all consulted friends who tried to sway us toward one or another solution for our lives, like my well-meaning buddy who couldn't imagine anyone accepting a job that didn't enhance earnings potential.

We can't make high-quality choices without making ourselves aware of disordered attachments that could cloud our judgment, and the very same principle applies to our friends, parents, and advisers. They won't behave like the pointer of a scale at equilibrium without knowing their own predispositions and attachments. Otherwise, instead of dispassionately listening to us, they will subconsciously tilt the scale to one side or the other.

These same principles apply not only in one-on-one settings but equally when groups make choices on behalf of their families, organizations, or business departments. On countless occasions in various countries I met with J. P. Morgan colleagues to decide how to allocate bonuses, or which business lines to grow, or how to economize in the face of a market downturn. In the end, those varied deliberations all boiled down to a common overriding objective: what would be best for the company and its shareholders. And lots of times, we all put aside self-interest and biases to focus only on that concern.

But in other cases, deliberations lapsed into Darwinian struggle sessions. Instead of dispassionately searching out the best course for our company, each of us dug in to defend his or her team, turf, or self-interest. Tough, outspoken colleagues browbeat those who might have had good ideas but lousy debating skills. Politically weak colleagues didn't dare cross politically well-connected ones. Squeaky wheels squeaked hard in their own self-interest. Such meetings sometimes convened the smartest people I had ever worked with, but we didn't always make the smartest choices. Why not? We didn't grasp Ignatius's wisdom that good friends, good family members, or good business teams have to check their disordered attachments at the door to start each deliberation like the pointer of a scale in equilibrium, free to weigh the data objectively and willing to offer truly disinterested advice.

Other spiritual traditions have developed practices that reflect this same rich wisdom. Quakers, for example, may convene a clearness committee in which a community member presents a looming personal decision to a small group of peers. The author Parker Palmer writes of using a clearness committee to help him ponder an offer to become a college president. His colleagues listened nonjudgmentally and didn't tell him what they thought he ought to do. But they did ask some pointed questions that helped Palmer scrutinize his motives and thought process. At one point, he had to admit that what he was most looking forward to about the job was "getting my picture in the paper with the word *president* under it." With that sheepish admission, "it was obvious, even to me," Palmer continues, "that my desire to be president had much more to do with ego" than with a deep desire to contribute to the world through that position. The clearness committee accomplished their goal by helping Palmer clarify his thinking, become aware of unhealthy attachments, and weed out shoddy reasoning.[16]

Whether as spiritual directors, parents, bosses, or members of Quaker-style clearness committees, good advisers and mentors realize that it's your journey, not theirs, and they help you make it well. An outsider's perspective is invaluable as we wade through facts, feelings, and conflicted thoughts that surface while we're in the throes of complicated decisions. Friends might see considerations that we've overlooked, force us to confront truths we're denying, or play our feelings back to us in language that crystallizes an emerging pattern of thinking.

For such reasons, Ignatius of Loyola instructed every Jesuit to consult a spiritual director regularly, a rule that has applied even to those many Jesuits who ended up becoming saints. Who is going to give good advice to a saint? Well, the best advisers excel not because they are holier than we are, but because they are willing to listen, understand their own attachments and ferret out ours, speak honestly, and let us live our own lives rather than manipulate us.

Mentors with those skills are invaluable, whether they are great saints or great sinners.

Another critical trait characterizes Ignatian-style mentors. An early guidebook to the *Spiritual Exercises* says that good directors should "never display the slightest sign of discouragement or annoyance, but encourage and stiffen the [counselee] to perseverance."[17] Perseverance is often exactly what is needed when pondering complicated choices that involve many apparent pros and cons.

Can you think of situations in the workplace where colleagues brought their agendas to the table in a way that resulted in bad business decisions? Or examples in your personal life where you were given agenda-driven advice?

Who do you know that serves as a wise mentor, spiritual director, or decision-making coach? What attributes characterize the way they help your decision-making process?

Do It Over Again and Again— by Using Multiple Perspectives

Any decision-making process that harnesses our emotions can feel as spooky and unreliable as consulting a psychic for our next career move. Even Ignatius, a champion of the inner voice, knew that feelings can mislead or be misinterpreted, which is why we should double-check with the head what feels right to the heart; "It is in this way, namely, according to the greater motion arising from reason, and not according to some motion arising from sensitive human nature, that I ought to come to my decision" (#182).

But our heads are not perfect tools either. That's why it can help to ask the same question in different ways, because each perspective sheds new light and helps point us toward the right decision.

Before I worked in investment banking, I used to read about big merger deals and wonder what little black box told the bankers that a company was worth, say, $89 a share (why not $90 or $88?). Well, there is no magic black box; rather, acquisition specialists typically zero in on a purchase price by employing various valuation methods that generate a range of possible answers ($100 a share in one case, and $75, $90, and $87 in others). Each method is rational, but none yields a definitive answer. The bankers ultimately make a judgment call, and they gain greater confidence in their judgment by exploring their valuation problem from multiple perspectives.

Ignatius had the same insight about our personal choices. We will choose more wisely and confidently by looking at dilemmas from multiple perspectives. Often, when we can't easily reach a decision about a personal matter, we keep rehashing the matter through the same exact thought process; that's like banging our heads against a wall—it will produce a headache but little new insight. Instead, Ignatius suggests pondering the same question through various approaches, such as the following three.

Weigh the pros and cons: "I should consider the advantages and benefits . . . and contrarily the disadvantages and dangers" (#181). When faced with a choice between two alternatives, jot down the perceived pros and cons of each one. That discipline alone sometimes turns a vexing decision into an easy one. When we first ponder a looming choice, the pros and cons may swirl around in a confusing mental muddle, but once we wrestle them onto paper and organize them into columns, the reasons may pile up so disproportionately on one side of the ledger that the right choice seems completely clear. Whether or not a clear answer seems to be developing from that approach, an Ignatian-style decision maker might then mull the same decision from a very different perspective.

Imagine that you're giving advice to someone else who shares your dilemma: "I will imagine a person whom I have never seen or known." What advice would you give that person, "desiring all perfection for him or her" (#185)? It's often easier to advise others than to advise ourselves! Most of us have been pained at some point to see friends stuck in miserable relationships or dead-end jobs. We wonder why what's so obvious to us remains lost to them. Well, we usually know why they don't see the need to change, because we've been in their shoes: mired in denial, stuck in a rut, afraid of change, or lacking the perspective to see what's obvious from an objective distance. So, we might gain better perspective on our own choices if we imagine that we are trying to advise a friend in a similar situation.

Ignatius then suggests another imaginative exercise. Imagine how you will look at this situation from your deathbed and what decision you will wish you had made: "I will consider, as if I were at the point of death, what procedure and norm I will at that time wish I had used in the manner of making the present election" (#186). Anyone plagued by gnawing regrets over a past decision will understand why this intimidating mental exercise can be effective. No one wants to look back over his or her life and suffer regrets, particularly not from a deathbed when no time remains to make amends.

So, Ignatius suggests, decide now to manage your life business in ways that will avoid regrets in old age. The American naturalist Henry David Thoreau retreated to Walden Pond to ponder his life and its course because, he says, he didn't want "when I came to die, to discover that I had not lived."[18]

This deathbed decision technique brings to mind a biblically wise anecdote in comedian Steve Martin's *New Yorker* reminiscence of his father. Although their relationship had been strained for years, Martin had slowly begun wedging open the lines of communication late in his father's life. Martin recalls sitting beside his father who lay dying, the two gazing at each other in silence for some time. Both understood this could be the last of their earthly meetings. After some time in silence, Martin's father said, "I wish I could cry, I wish I could cry for all the love I received and couldn't return."[19] The episode poignantly illustrates the power of contemplating looming choices as if on one's deathbed.

The episode also reinforces the value of aligning major life choices to our purpose: Steve Martin's dying father was measuring his life against a beautiful, worthy mission: to give as much love as he had received. The dying man might have regretted not executing this mission as well as he wished he would have. (I suspect, though, that anyone sensitive enough to ponder such a question in life's waning hours might well have given plenty of love along the way.)

The lesson learned from Ignatius of Loyola and Steve Martin's father (God rest him): avoid regrets late in life by pondering major choices as if looking back over your life. The nineteenth-century Danish philosopher Søren Kierkegaard once said, "Life is lived forward, but understood backward." Ignatius is trying to turn this plain wisdom into a proactive tool by imaginatively putting us in position to look back and understand how we would like to have lived but before we go out and do the living.

Make Your Choices—Risks and All

We all know people with a gift for making sound choices. A handful of my former J. P. Morgan colleagues, esteemed for uncannily good judgment, were regularly consulted about matters far removed from their area of business expertise. We asked them to interview and assess prospective new hires; we sought their input on contemplated reorganizations of business lines; we consulted them about our career paths. We trusted their judgment because we had seen how well they seemed to manage decisions about their own lives and careers.

These folks would mull major decisions, sometimes for a few minutes and sometimes for a few days, until they became comfortable with a choice. They themselves might not know exactly what internal process had left them tranquil and committed after pressured and difficult deliberations. They may have intuitively mastered much of the art that Ignatius calls, in its totality, "discernment of spirits"—they retreated to go forward by creating time and space to weigh important decisions; they scrutinized their thought process to be sure they weren't pressured or swayed by their own or colleagues' personal agendas (or attachments); they paid attention to their gut feel and comfort level with their choice (as if testing for a feeling approximating consolation). They checked whether the prospective choice lined up with their long-term purpose and their values.

The good news is that these expert decision makers' good judgment is not some mysterious power—an X factor as the *Harvard Business Review* called it—but a human skill that can be taught and developed. Ignatius lends some insight and rigorous methodology as to what the X factor involves and how we might use it reliably and systematically when we make decisions.

Decision-making tools have proliferated greatly since Ignatius's day, particularly in the last half century or so. Occupational psychologists have developed personality inventories and job-preference tools; self-help books for "dummies" have given us step-by-step guides to everything from switching careers to finding mates; business consultants have taught us about force-field analysis and making a SWOT analysis (an anagram reminding us to examine our strengths, weaknesses, opportunities, and threats when formulating a strategy). The Jesuit founder would undoubtedly be delighted to see how we've expanded our arsenal of decision-making tools and would encourage us to make good use of them.

But he would likely be saddened that we've slowly lost touch with our own inner wisdom. In *Judgment: How Winning Leaders Make Great Calls*, Noel Tichy and Warren Bennis, both outstanding leadership thinkers, note how internal factors can impair good judgment. "We all have blindnesses. We get attached to people. We distort the facts. We look the other way." [20] They're right on all counts, and let's not forget greed, fear of change, shortsightedness, or the countless other debilitating attachments chronicled in this chapter.

But the decision-making process these authors prescribe does not include a solution for the harmful inner attachments they describe. Ignatius, in contrast, understood that our attachments are frequently the prime culprits behind bad decisions and that no decision-making process will work unless it taps our inner wisdom and resources to combat inner attachments. No tool, decision-making checklist, Web site, or guidebook will ever replace the willingness to listen to our inner voice, the ability to hear it, and the skill to interpret it by using head and heart as mutual checks and balances:

- Don't just look at the facts; check to see that no biases or predispositions (disordered attachments) are subtly swaying your interpretation of those facts.

- Don't brainstorm your alternatives without also making yourself emotionally and spiritually free to expose and pursue all legitimate courses of action.

- Don't rely on your reasoning process alone; bounce your thoughts off a wise friend who will offer objective, disinterested feedback.

- Don't ignore your inner voice; track consolations and desolations, because your heart can sometimes point you in the right direction before your head catches on.

We cannot choose correctly all the time. That plain fact inhibits many of us from making as many choices, and bold choices, as we ought to. Particularly prone to choice phobia are smart people who excelled in school and have ever since imagined that the real world would be similar to that setting. They shrink from making choices where an A—a good result—isn't clearly in sight. Fear of failing or of looking foolish becomes a subtle but driving disordered affection behind their reluctance to make big choices.

The story goes that Pope John XXIII's personal secretary strenuously attempted to dissuade the pope from convening the Second Vatican Council, fearing that the momentous initiative would prove disastrous and taint the pope's legacy. The pope's reply to his reluctant secretary reveals a profound mastery of discernment as Ignatius understood it: "You're still not detached enough from self. You're still concerned with having a good reputation. Only when the ego has been trampled underfoot can one be fully and truly free."[21] Think of it this way: only when you are free to risk failure are you free to risk success.

Early in my investment banking career, I was shocked to hear a manager criticize a talented subordinate by saying, "Take more risk!" The subordinate was hesitant to rely on his judgment, and the manager wanted him to generate greater revenue by showing more confidence and taking more risk in his trading choices.

Up to that moment, *risk* had been a bad word. Parents and teachers warned against taking risks; risk resulted in skinned knees, afterschool detention, broken toys, and visits to hospital emergency rooms. "Take more risk" was the mantra of the pitchfork-wielding demon permanently perched on my left shoulder while the whiteshrouded angel perched atop my other shoulder steered hard in the other direction.

But in life, as on that J. P. Morgan trading floor, we often profit only by taking appropriate risk. We risk failure with every marriage proposal, job change, relocation to a new city, or choice of one college major over another. In fact, in some cases, the odds of failure will be greater than the odds of success, as every successful entrepreneur knows when launching a start-up venture. Indeed, Ignatius of Loyola took enormous personal risk in cofounding the Jesuits, at the time a revolutionary new kind of religious order that began with no capital, minimal political support, and very uncertain prospects.

A mentor once told me that the best thing to happen in his career was botching the first major decision he faced. The best thing? Yes, he said. Life went on, he picked himself up, he survived, and he learned that we can often correct mistakes and that life frequently offers second and third chances—not always chances to undo past mistakes but chances to do other good things. So, from that time, he was never afraid to make a decision and never afraid to take personal risk. He lived proactively and modeled a world-loving, world-embracing attitude.

We can't fulfill our purpose in the world without taking risk and making choices. Our purpose, vision, and values may be our enduring beacons through life, the "port to which we are sailing," as Seneca put it. But our talents, circumstances, resources, and interests will all change through life, as will the world we live in.

In fact, our choices are the only bridge between where we stand now and the port to which we want to head. Choices are the only path from the civilization we've inherited to the civilization we aspire to create.

Choose wisely.

Choose Wisely
Learn to use your head and your heart.
» Listen to the still, small voice.

9
—

Live in Freedom
Listen to the Still, Small Voice

The previous chapter outlined practices that fortify us to make wise decisions. We need to assess our ever-changing talents, circumstances, and resources. We need to read consolations and desolations and to free ourselves from greed, pride, fear, or other disordered affections that could sway us toward misguided choices.

But freedom from shortsighted attachments must be complemented by farsighted vision of where we want to go. That is, freedom from attachments becomes truly strategic only when it's freedom for a worthy purpose. Sharp decision-making skills matter only when they serve a mission or vision. It's no surprise, then, that Ignatius of Loyola similarly urged freedom from crippling, self-absorbed attachments to promote freedom for a very lofty life purpose.

All over the world, that lofty purpose is memorialized in stained-glass windows, emblazoned on emblems, and chiseled into building cornerstones: AMDG. Those letters stand for *ad majorem Dei gloriam*: "for God's greater glory." That motto surfaces throughout Jesuit documents and inspires good works all over the globe. Ignatius counseled that we are well positioned to confront a major choice only once we have rendered ourselves emotionally free to pursue all legitimate courses of action. At that point, he says, we ought "to choose that which is more to the glory of the Divine Majesty" (#152). That same standard ought to govern all our life

choices. Whether choosing careers or spouses, what to do in retirement, or how to spend our money, we ought to make ourselves free
and then choose what is AMDG.

With those four letters, questions that lay between the lines in
previous chapters now blink in neon: What is God asking of us?
What does it mean to make choices that reflect God's greater glory?
Or if we're here on earth to be holy, repair the world, build the civilization of love, or struggle for the kingdom, just how much repairing, building, or struggling is enough? A good deed now and then?
A generous gift to the church offering plate every Sunday? An occasional weekend of volunteer work? Or a fully dedicated lifetime?

We sometimes speak of God's plan for our lives or use words like
vocation or *calling*. If we are in fact being called, someone must be
doing the calling. So, is God calling us? And, if so, what is God
calling us to do?

Which Work Glorifies God?

Once upon a time, it was easier for Christians to answer such questions. Ignatius was typical of sixteenth-century Catholics in advis-
ing, "We should strongly praise religious institutes, virginity and
continence, and marriage too, but not as highly as any of the former"
(#356). The worthiest Christian calling was understood to be the
priesthood or religious life; next came virginal lay life, and bringing
up the godly rear were all those who got married and, presumably,
supported their families with paid work in the secular world.

No mainstream Catholic nowadays, starting with the pope, would
suggest that a priestly vocation excels that of a married person.
Ironically, today's Catholic catechism would faintly echo Ignatius's
ideological sparring partner, the reformer Martin Luther, in proclaiming that all of us are called to be holy, and all legitimate states
of life and work are paths to holiness. We homemakers, office administrators, janitors, and others can find comfort in Luther's assurance
that "what you do in your house is worth as much as if you did it up in

heaven for our Lord God."[1] And even though a dedicated father who changes the diapers at night might be ridiculed by his buddies as an "effeminate fool" (in Luther's words), "God," Luther continued, "with all his angels and creatures, is smiling." All legitimate work, if done with faithfulness, service, and love, is equally pleasing to God.[2]

Some of Luther's reformer colleagues went on to say that instead of worrying about whether one job is better, more important, or worthier than another, we should simply rejoice in our livelihood as God's will for us and pursue it conscientiously. John Calvin claimed that "[the Lord] has appointed duties for every man in his particular way of life. And . . . [God] has named these various kinds of living 'callings.' Therefore each individual has his own kind of living assigned to him by the Lord as a sort of sentry post that he may not heedlessly wander about throughout life."[3]

That sentiment may have consoled the carpenters and bakers of Calvin's day. But most of them had few career choices to begin with, as they frequently inherited a parent's livelihood and pursued it from late childhood until they reached death's door. Many of us, on the other hand, face far more occupational choices, not to mention a long, productive retirement. And if God indeed has appointed a career sentry post for any of us, we'll have a tough time manning that post through the downsizings, layoffs, outsourcings, and other endemic workplace calamities of the present.

Our Most Basic Responsibility

We live and work in a radically different world from what Ignatius, Luther, or Calvin could have foreseen. And so, as we make our way from one job to another, the conscientious among us sometimes wonder whether we are doing what God would want us to be doing. I've found that question addressed unambiguously in only one Scripture verse, where the prophet Micah proclaims, "What does the Lord require of you but to do justice, and to love kindness, and to walk humbly with your God?" (6:8).

Micah seems to reinforce one of our fundamental points: in a constantly changing world, the first question is no longer, What job will I do? but, What kind of person will I be? And Micah echoes previous chapters in calling us to be people of mighty purpose and noble values, people who do justice and love kindness, whatever our profession or state of life.

Jesus' observations of a poor widow add a further dimension to Micah's wisdom. Jesus "sat down opposite the treasury, and watched the crowd putting money into the treasury. Many rich people put in large sums. A poor widow came and put in two small copper coins, which are worth a penny." Jesus praises the woman, contrasting her to the well-respected, wealthy notables who donate to charity some sliver of their wealth, in part to win the adulation of their community. He explains that these people contribute "out of their abundance." Although greatly talented, they are small spirited in every sense of the word.

But this poor widow can scrape together only a meager donation to the temple. Jesus points out that she, "out of her poverty has put in everything she had, all she had to live on." She is great spirited and praiseworthy for it (Mark 12:41–44).

So what is God asking of us, and what might it mean to make choices for God's greater glory? A simple answer arises from the poor widow's example. We are asked to put everything we have into it (paraphrasing Jesus) by giving deeply from the very substance of our time, money, energy, intellect, and many other talents, and not to glorify ourselves by serving ourselves, but to give greater glory to God by serving God's people.

Thunderbolts and Lightning?

Yet even if I'm putting my all into it and trying to follow Micah's instruction to walk humbly with my God, I am still left to wonder whether God would prefer that I walk as a banker, teacher, lawyer, or priest. After all, Scripture beguiles us with stories in which

God expresses irresistible and unmistakably clear opinions about job choices. Jesus called the fishermen Simon and Andrew, "and immediately they left their nets and followed him," abandoning one life strategy for a radically different one (Mark 1:18). In an even more dramatic New Testament episode, "light from heaven flashed around" the future apostle Paul. In case those divine pyro-technics didn't get Paul's attention, he was also knocked to the ground, blinded, and summoned by a heavenly voice to "get up and enter the city, and you will be told what you are to do" (Acts 9:3–4, 6).

He got the point, and we probably would too if God's plan for our lives were made so compellingly clear. This book would be much shorter if I could bottle that formula for personal strategic clarity. But we don't often hear voices or see light from heaven flashing around us, and we are probably wise to regard skeptically those who claim they do. We sometimes stumble around in the semidarkness. Now and then, we knowingly make dreadful choices, consumed by greed, lust, anger, fear, or a hundred other private demons. We make other bad choices unwittingly, wanting to choose well but not see-ing the right path. And often, even when we've made pretty good choices, we can't tell with certainty that we've chosen the very best path and found our calling, so to speak. We feel not like the Paul who enjoyed lightning-bolt clarity but like the Paul who once said, "Now I see as through a glass, darkly" (1 Corinthians 13:12).

Maybe those stories of unmistakable clarity do us a disservice by feeding the idea that God typically screams in thunderbolts or advertises with lightning strikes. It seems that, for the most part, God speaks more subtly—which makes perfect sense. After all, if we ought to reverence each person's human dignity, surely God expresses that virtue above all by respecting our freedom to chart our unique paths toward building the civilization of love.

But if God respects our freedom (and no doubt delights in what-ever creative, ingenious choices we make), God, like a good friend or loving parent, might nonetheless subtly indicate what choices

will make us happy and effective. That's certainly what Ignatius of
Loyola believed. His various decision tools might have struck readers as making lots of common sense, but Ignatius saw more than
common sense at work in them. To be sure, he wanted to help
sharpen our wits, but he didn't believe we were relying on our wits
alone and so advised us to begin every important decision process
with prayer for enlightenment: "I should beg God our Lord to be
pleased to move my will and to put into my mind what I ought to
do in regard to the matter proposed" (#180).

Furthermore, when Ignatius urged mentors to conduct themselves like the pointer of a scale in equilibrium, it wasn't merely to
secure their impartiality but "to allow the Creator to deal immediately with the creature" (#15). A privileged and prayerful communication may take place between God and someone pondering
a life choice, and the last thing a mentor should do is meddle in
that conversation. As Ignatius saw it, God most often communi-
cates not through lightning bolts, voices in our heads, miracles, or
angelic appearances, but in the consolations that confirm we're on
the right path and the desolations that alert us to trouble. Those
consolations, Ignatius says, are not earth-shattering sensations, but
"touch the soul gently, lightly, and sweetly, like a drop of water
going into a sponge" (#335). Ignatius was, in part, echoing the
apostle Paul, who likewise said that the "fruit of the Spirit is love,
joy, peace, patience, kindness, generosity, faithfulness, gentleness,
and self-control" (Galatians 5:22–23).

The Voice "in Here"

The Hebrew prophet Elijah finds God speaking in similar ways.
We're told that Elijah witnessed a "great wind, so strong that it
was splitting mountains and breaking rocks in pieces." But Elijah
perceived that "the Lord was not in the wind," or in the earthquake
or fires that followed. Instead, later on, there was a "sound of sheer

silence." And Elijah heard God speak out of that silence. Those of us who heard this story as children may remember the poetic King James language for this encounter—Elijah heard God's "still small voice" (1 Kings 19:11–13).

Perhaps, if we attune ourselves to hearing that still, small voice, we will find it whispered all around us and, more important, from within us. As the Quaker minister Parker Palmer put it, "Vocation does not come from a voice 'out there' calling me to become something I am not. It comes from a voice 'in here' calling me to be the person I was born to be, to fulfill the original selfhood given me at birth by God."[4]

And just how might we recognize the voice "in here"? The Protestant minister Frederick Buechner hears God communicating to us through our profoundest human concerns and interests: "The place that God calls us is that place where the world's deep hunger and our own deep desire meet."[5] And one of my friends, asked how God might influence our job choices, said she saw God's fingerprint on our skills and circumstances: "The gifts and talents God has given us are clues as to God's plan for us." Another friend spoke similarly, focusing on the passions and interests that not only motivate us to excellence but also touch all those who see our excellence in action: "What fuels one to perform with excellence has a spiritual quality that inspires, nurtures, and sustains one's work. . . . I find when I experience extraordinary talent in someone—whether it is playing tennis, singing, preaching, caring for the sick—it reminds me of God's grace and seems to be a very wonderful way for that person to use his or her time and energy."

Anywhere that friend sees human excellence devoted to a worthy end, she sees God at work. Similarly, the nineteenth-century Jesuit poet Gerard Manley Hopkins found God's voice and presence in countless everyday encounters: "For Christ plays in ten thousand places, / Lovely in limbs, and lovely in eyes not his."[6]

Perhaps God also speaks through our circumstances, life's unpredictable, unexpected turns that eventually convince all but the most stubborn of us what Fr. Ciszek eventually learned while sitting in that jail cell in Soviet Russia: we don't control as much of life as we imagined when we were invincible twenty-year-olds. We learn the truth of Jesus' haunting prediction to the apostle Peter: "When you were younger, you used to fasten your own belt and to go wherever you wished. But when you grow old, you will stretch out your hands, and someone else will fasten a belt around you and take you where you do not wish to go" (John 21:18). Scripture scholars interpret that melancholy verse as the Gospel writer's attempt to explain Peter's gruesome martyrdom as something other than a total disaster for the fledgling, uncertain Christian community.

But who hasn't lived Peter's mystery in some small way? We find ourselves less in control of our destinies than we once imagined. Career plans don't work out; bodies don't respond as they once did; unforeseen tragedies, deaths of loved ones, and marital breakups shatter cherished dreams. Some dreams are not merely deferred but die.

Yet remarkably other doors open and other possibilities emerge. We find new ways to make our way forward in the world. Like Ignatius of Loyola, whose dreams of a military career shattered along with his leg, we stand up eventually and walk again. Indeed, our passage through disappointment and trauma can seem, in retrospect, a season of grace. We struggled back to our feet by our own courage and determination, but we also felt an empowering touch, as when Jesus reached out to a death-struck young girl and exhorted, "'Talitha cum,' which means, 'Little girl, get up!'" (Mark 5:41). We do get up, and in the course of a subsequent lifetime, we often walk farther and climb higher than we first imagined possible. We see that great personal tragedies bear not only sorrow but sometimes the seeds of our own resurrections.

How are we to interpret the alternately serendipitous and disappointing, unexpected and unpredictable, courses of our lives? What is happening when death or financial disaster force us to reconsider what we want from life, when teachers or mentors find and nurture talent we didn't know we had, when we succeed beyond our wildest imaginings, when managers steer our careers in fortuitous directions, when we aren't offered the job we wanted so badly, when friends point out opportunities that we didn't know existed, or when we persist in pursuing a personal passion against all odds of success, only to find that success and fulfillment eventually come? Do such cases merely vindicate human ingenuity, resilience, fortitude, and imagination? Or is God, too, at work in some ineffable way, as Hopkins says, "play[ing] in ten thousand places / Lovely in limbs, and lovely in eyes not his"?

Well, why not both? That's how I read Ignatius, the former military commander and take-charge, type-A personality who nonetheless attuned himself to read God's will in the subtle promptings of consolations and desolations. Or, as expressed in a great mantra of Jesuit spirituality, "Find God in all things."

The Burning Bush

If we attune ourselves to look and listen, we may find God present within us, all around us, and speaking to us constantly. But if we don't bother to look, it will seem that there is nothing to be seen. Here's how the nineteenth-century British poet Elizabeth Barrett Browning wryly described humans, who so often miss what lies plainly in front of us:

> Earth's crammed with heaven,
> And every common bush afire with God;
> But only he who sees, takes off his shoes—
> The rest sit round it and pluck blackberries.[7]

The poet is alluding to the Exodus story in which Moses, encountering God in a burning bush, removes his sandals and hears the call to lead his people out of slavery and into the Promised Land.

The overarching question of this chapter—what is God calling us to do?—is answered before that burning bush. Like Moses, we are first of all called to recognize that we live and work and stand in a holy place, "a world charged with the grandeur of God."[8] We are called, therefore, to the holiness that Rabbi Kushner earlier defined as "being aware that [we] are in the presence of God."[9]

We are called, further, to freedom from whatever shackles us. For Moses' people, it was freedom from oppression at the hands of an Egyptian pharaoh; for us, it may be getting over ourselves by breaking free from attachment to money, power, greed, fear, alcohol, sex, pride, prejudice, or any other demons that prevent our becoming our best selves.

We are called not only to freedom from something but to freedom for some mighty purpose. Like Moses, we are called to lead ourselves and our brothers and sisters toward a promised land. And we won't lead well without a clear vision of where we want to head, the kind of world we want to create, a civilization marked by "the greater magnificence of human virtue, people's goodness, collective prosperity, and true civilization: the civilization of love."[10]

Moses's call was particular to his time, life, and circumstances, and so is ours. Each of us will bring different talents and resources, live in unique circumstances, and consequently build the civilization of love in our particular way. We figure out our way forward by learning to choose well, and we will choose better still if we keep our eyes open to "every common bush afire with God" and our ears open to what Elijah called God's "still small voice" and our inner senses attuned to the consolations that "touch the soul gently, lightly, and sweetly, like a drop of water going into a sponge."

Have you ever experienced a still, small voice as you considered job or family decisions?

Do you have a sense of vocation or calling about any aspects of your life? If so, how would you describe that calling?

Create New Strategy for a New Time
Navigate a complex and fast-changing world.
Create strategy for your whole life.

Discover Your Mighty Purpose
Evaluate the world you've inherited.
Envision the future worth fighting for.
Articulate a purpose worth living for.
Embrace values worth standing for.
Put heart into strategy to give it life.

Choose Wisely
Learn to use your head and your heart.
Listen to the still, small voice.

PART FOUR

Make Every Day Matter

Get the mind-set for getting results.
Use a spiritual technology for purposeful living.

Make Every Day Matter
» Get the mind-set for getting results.
Use a spiritual technology for purposeful living.

1 0

Develop Consistency
Get the Mind-set for Getting Results

A very Johnson knows how to deliver superior performance. He won a National Basketball Association championship as a star player with the San Antonio Spurs and years later was named an NBA coach of the year for his ability to motivate others to excellence. Only a handful of basketball veterans can boast those twin achievements. Asked by the *New York Times* to explain his success secrets, Johnson cited a famed verse from Proverbs: "Without vision, the people perish."[1]

But vision alone accomplishes nothing. As Johnson said in the same interview, "I can talk about having a lot of faith or vision, but how early do I get to the office? How prepared am I going into the game? How much time do I spend with my players away from basketball, getting to know them better?" Those tasks and thousands of others like them are the stuff of execution: getting results, implementing plans, and turning vision into reality every day of the week. Execution is the nitty-gritty of doing all that. Or, as the subtitle of a best-selling book proclaims, execution is "the discipline of getting things done."

Often, we don't get things done for the simple reason that we don't focus intently on what we should actually be doing. We aspire to lofty goals but don't figure out what to do tomorrow and the next day to make those goals reality. As a result, February is littered with broken New Year's resolutions to lose weight, apply to graduate school, quit smoking, or stop wasting time. And Monday is littered with Sunday's already unfulfilled prayers to live a better life. More than once in my business career did colleagues and I end arduous strategy meetings by congratulating ourselves for hashing through tough, divisive issues and reaching consensus on some bold, new direction. We thought the hard part was deciding our strategic direction (or "choosing wisely," as the previous chapter put it). We were kidding ourselves! In fact, the hard part had just begun. Each of us became absorbed in our day-to-day travails; thus, no one followed up aggressively on our newly charted path; no one checked up painstakingly; and not much happened with our bold plan. No execution.

Military officers sometimes joke, "Strategy is for amateurs; implementation is for professionals." Well, soldiers certainly do face unique obstacles to successful execution. It's one thing to concoct a master battle plan in a calm situation room; it's quite another to implement that plan while bullets whiz past your head and opposing forces don't behave as planned. As a disciple of the famed nineteenth-century German military strategist Carl von Clausewitz once put it, "No plan survives first contact with the enemy." Real professionals can process information in real time, stay cool when others panic, and adhere to their mission and values even while improvising in response to upsets and surprises. Fortunately, most of us don't have to execute our life plans while facing hails of bullets. But life presents many unexpected upsets, surprises, and opportunities that constantly test our skills to get things done.

That's why any successful strategy needs to encompass all three dimensions of this book: the transformative power of vision and purpose; the ability to make good choices in an ever-changing world; and, now in this chapter, the skill to make every day matter.

Sir, I'm Putting a Man on the Moon

In 1959, Soviet engineers put into orbit *Sputnik*, a satellite brimming with about as much computing firepower as today's $10 digital

wristwatches. But at the time, Sputnik carried devastating psychological and symbolic power. Americans feared that their technological superiority was slipping away to the cold war archenemy,
the Soviet Union.

President John F. Kennedy later responded with the auda-
cious goal of putting a man on the moon by the end of the 1960s.
Sometime later, so the story goes, the president visited space agency
headquarters to assess progress and bolster the morale of slide-rule-
toting engineers who, improbably, were suddenly shouldering a
nation's self-confidence. The president crossed paths with a janitor
sweeping up an office and politely inquired about the gentleman's
job responsibilities. The janitor supposedly replied, "Mr. President,
I'm putting a man on the moon."

As simplistic and sentimental as that sounds, the man's remark
highlights a valid point: whether at NASA or on the high school
basketball court, a team performs best when individuals get over
themselves to embrace a mission greater than any one person can
accomplish. Alignment around a meaningful purpose invariably
makes individuals and teams more productive.

But however eloquent, clear, and compelling President Kennedy's
vision, the real challenge was making it happen. Think of the
thousands—millions?—of bite-sized tasks and objectives that were
enumerated, sequenced, and delivered year after year to put a man
on the moon. We like to mock the engineers and bureaucrats who
worry about the day-to-day stuff, but without them we wouldn't
have put a man on the moon in the 1960s, or yet.

Running our lives may not be as complicated as putting astronauts on the moon. But we face a challenge President Kennedy did
not. He articulated a vision, and countless others executed it. We,
in contrast, are fully accountable for playing both roles for our own
lives. To do those very different tasks well, we need to work out of
two seemingly opposite yet complementary attitudes described by
Microsoft chief executive Steve Ballmer: "You've got to be very
realistic about where you are, but very optimistic about where you
can be."[2] Or, more poetically:

A vision without a task is but a dream,

A task without vision is drudgery,

A vision and a task is a hope of the world.

(Attributed to a church in England, 1730.)

How Not to Get Things Done

When we consider getting things done from year to year and day to day, we might think of to-do lists, checklists, and, in business circles, operating plans. Is there a duller topic than operating plans? It bores me even to write the phrase, which conjures up images of bureaucratic gnomes bearing thick reports that everyone else ignores. A former J. P. Morgan colleague once described an internal meeting convened to discuss expense overruns against the annual operating plan. After the various business managers were assembled, the department's designated expense tracker scuttled in, laden with so many reports that he had to wheel them in on a dolly. The senior manager running the meeting pointed to the reams of paper and said, "Don't tell me that's the solution, because *that's* the problem." Everyone had a good laugh at the poor bureaucrat's expense, the tension broke, and the assembled business managers got to do what well-paid managers often do: find a way to blame someone else (the poor accountant, in this case) for the financial mess that they themselves had created.

Well, the senior manager was right about this much: the solution to execution problems lies not in better organized and more detailed piles of paper. Although we're well intentioned in our personal plans, New Year's resolutions, and other assorted lists, our paper plans usually float along in a parallel universe, disconnected from our day-to-day reality.

This story illustrates why we don't live out our plans and visions. Like those business managers, we often lose track of something important (in their case, living within a budget) because we have too many other things to worry about. Or we avoid confronting what is difficult and unpleasant (like budgets) and are drawn to distractions that are more exciting and appealing. And like those business managers, when we do foul up, we sometimes try to shift to someone else the blame for our misdeeds. All that means:

- We don't focus enough on the most important things.
- We take on too many tasks at once.
- We don't vigilantly track how things are going.
- We don't accept full accountability for our actions.

Sometimes we paper over these problems (literally) with to-do lists and operating plans, but we can't paper over the root issues—we need to deal with them head-on. To help us do so, I've assembled an unlikely panel of execution experts: a saint, a megacorporation, some self-confessed alcoholics, one of my neighbors, and a former boss.

Where do your day-to-day efforts to get things done habitually run into difficulties?

Focus: Learn from St. John Berchmans

Jesuit trainees are routinely encouraged to study the saints and emulate their heroism. One such role model is the Belgian Jesuit St. John Berchmans, who died at age twenty-two after contracting a fever. He was later lionized as one of three Jesuit boyhood saints, together with Aloysius Gonzaga and Stanislaus Kostka, two other Jesuits who died at tragically young ages.

Unfortunately, in the biographies written after their deaths, the three men lose the fleshy toughness that made them distinctively human and truly holy. Typically depicted as a trio in church paintings and statuary, their unblemished and virtually indistinguishable faces gaze serenely heavenward in saccharine poses that isolate them from the rest of us mortals. The *Catholic Encyclopedia* informs us that young Berchmans was "a favourite with his playmates, brave and open, attractive in manner, and with a bright, joyful disposition."[3] One or two readers may recognize their eight-year-old selves in that description, but most of us certainly won't.

But the very next sentence hints that John Berchmans was human after all. We're informed that he was "by natural disposition, impetuous and fickle." Even real human beings, with all our foibles, can be saintly. And Berchmans's circumstances and upbringing were more real than what we read in some histories. Unlike the other boyhood saints, Gonzaga and Kostka, he did not descend from nobility. He grew up in a normal household headed by a shoemaker father. And his family confronted the same challenges that us non-nobles frequently face, such as paying for our kids' tuitions. His cash-strapped father had to inform the thirteen-year-old Berchmans that he would have to leave school and apprentice to the shoe business to help support the family. But Berchmans was feeling called to help souls rather than cobble soles. He made a deal with his parents, taking a position as the house servant for a local priest to raise a little money while pursuing minor seminary studies. He entered the Jesuit novitiate not long after.

During my short but happy Jesuit career, a superior once told us trainees an anecdote about Berchmans playing billiards one evening with other novices. As Berchmans lined up a shot, some holier-than-thou fellow novice glided by, presumably on his way to chapel, and asked, "Brother Berchmans, what would you do if you knew the world would end in a minute?" The inquisitor surely intended to shame Berchmans into admitting that he, too, should be heading to chapel. Instead, the saint-to-be never shifted his eyes from the billiard table and replied, "What would I do? I would hit this shot as well as I could."

I have no way of knowing the story's authenticity. Maybe my superior made it up, resentful of those holier-than-thou portraits that do Berchmans no justice. Or if the story is true, other Jesuit novice directors probably don't appreciate its mixed message— what Jesuit superior wants young trainees goofing around rather than praying? But even if it's apocryphal, the story helps us get from putting a man on the moon to what we do today. It's a little story about focus. If you want to put a man on the moon, understand that you can't do much else at the same time, and so focus your effort where it counts. An earlier-quoted saying encouraged us *age quod agis*: do what you're doing! In other words, whatever is worth doing is worth doing excellently (including, I suppose, lining up the last billiard shot of your life). And no one will execute excellently if constantly distracted by other objectives or the desire to be doing something else.

The best business leaders I knew distinguished themselves, in part, by a willingness to make choices that focused energy, resources, and effort. The wishy-washy tried to cover their bases by doing and pursuing a little bit of everything, clearly fearful of committing to the wrong path; in the end, they succeeded only in diluting already-scarce resources and scattering their focus to the point of inefficiency. Great managers, on the other hand, made tough either-or choices that directed effort and talent toward a limited number of objectives.

Another Latin proverb adds a spiritual dimension to the point: *non multa sed multum*, or "not many things but much." Jesuits didn't coin that phrase, though I've heard it attributed to them, probably because its spirit so closely aligns with other Jesuit ideals. The quality with which a work is done—the "muchness" of it—can be more important than the sheer quantity of tasks a person completes. What value, for example, that a social worker counsels fifty people a day if each feels like a processed can rolling through an assembly line? Or what value is there in people parroting hundreds of prayers without real conscious engagement? We earlier quoted Archbishop Óscar Romero's take on this theme: "We cannot do everything and there is a sense of liberation in realizing that. This enables us to do something and do it very well." Or as Mother Teresa put it: "We cannot do great things on this earth; we can only do little things with great love."

And so this exhortation to focus is not only an enhancement to our spirituality but also a great help to our productivity. When I asked a subordinate to do one task, he or she would certainly remember and almost always deliver, and usually do it well. If I asked that same person to do ten things, a few would get lost in the clutter or be prioritized away. Almost invariably, one of us would be unhappy with the result, because I hadn't focused enough to help him or her focus. We can't manage other people that way, and we can't manage the business of our own lives that way either.

Focus on one thing at a time, and do it to the very best of your ability.

Get Real-Time Feedback and Make Real-Time Corrections: Learn from Walmart

Nothing is more crucial to retailers than the period between Thanksgiving and Christmas, when many merchants rack up fully one-third of total annual sales. Those few weeks often make the difference between annual profit and loss, and sometimes the difference between solvency and bankruptcy.

Retailers such as Walmart engage in high-stakes merchandising warfare to win foot traffic. Walmart might lure me with a ridiculously low price on a television, appliance, or this year's hot toy. The loss leader gets me in the door, and Walmart executives bet that I'll load my shopping cart with other, more profitably priced goods before checking out.

Executives hunker down at headquarters during this make-or-break selling season to scrutinize daily—even hourly—sales statistics pouring in from stores around the country, just as generals in command centers track reports from various battlefield sectors.

Well, a few days into a recent Christmas retailing battle, Walmart's generals realized they were losing their war. Advertising and promotional strategies had been meticulously planned for months, but "no plan survives first contact with the enemy." Competing retailers had crafted more enticing sales promotions and were winning foot traffic and sales away from Walmart.

Had the same scenario unfolded a decade or so earlier, before retailers developed real-time sales tracking technology, Walmart's selling season might have ended in disaster. Company executives would have groped around in semidarkness, relying on anecdotal evidence and sketchy results; by the time they fully came to grips with their unfurling disaster, it would have been early January and a bit too late to do much about the Christmas selling season. By the early twenty-first century, however, technology had advanced so that the company could access the needed information in real time. And the managers were courageous and resourceful enough to do something about it. They changed course rapidly by reshuffling the mix of sales items and promotions. It worked, and the selling season was salvaged.

As individuals, we, too, need to learn how to track our progress and adjust accordingly.

Gather feedback every day on how you're doing, and summon the courage and resourcefulness to change behavior in response to what you learn.

Break Large Challenges into Bite-Sized Ones: Learn from Alcoholics Anonymous

Have you kept your New Year's resolutions? Not if you're like most of us. We signed up for gym memberships on January 2 to buff our flabby physiques; by January 30 we were inquiring whether the annual membership fee was partly refundable. One noted psychologist has estimated that "80% of our resolutions have slipped by January 24." Why? "We make too many," he says, or "they are too long range and all encompassing."[4]

Consider, in contrast, some stellar resolution keepers: many thousands of people who have stopped drinking through the Alcoholics Anonymous program. I can't give up snacking on potato chips for a week; AA members often conquer the debilitating disease of alcoholism for a lifetime.

Its founder and proponents championed a program of twelve linked and interdependent steps. But one particular AA mantra helps explain why adherents execute their pledge to stop drinking and do it more effectively than most of us fulfill our New Year's resolutions. They aim never to drink again, but they worry only about today. Indeed, the AA mantra "One day at a time" has found its way into mainstream popular culture thanks to grateful program beneficiaries.

A lifetime is a daunting stretch of time for the human psyche to grasp. The alcoholic in addiction's throes might despair before the challenge of never taking a drink for years and years, but he or she just might be able to make it through today without a drink, and then wake up tomorrow and, with a bit more confidence, get through that day without a drink. You stop drinking for the rest of your life by not drinking today, by learning to live one day at time.

Likewise, NASA put a man on the moon by figuring out what had to be done one day at a time. The same holds for every ambitious goal and for lofty values such as integrity, reverence, or excellence: accomplish them one day at a time.

And if one day at a time is too ambitious a goal, break ambitious goals into even more manageable steps. The New York Mets pitcher Orlando Hernández, once asked about his game plan after a masterful seven-inning performance, said, "I don't look at seven innings. I look at it one inning at a time, three outs. I get through that inning. I look at the next inning."[5]

Break large challenges into bite-sized ones, check every day on how you're doing, and let today's success propel you into tomorrow.

Remind Yourself Daily What You Care About: Learn from My Neighbor

Some 8 million of us live in New York City, and we've gotten used to living in close quarters. My apartment in a high-rise building overlooks the terraces of a neighboring high-rise. Like most New Yorkers, I've grown accustomed to my own compromised privacy and a bit nosy about the dramas that might unfold in my neighbors' lives. Will I, like Jimmy Stewart in *Rear Window*, someday spy a neighbor trying to cover up a murder? Probably not. The most drama I'll glimpse will likely be a heated argument or a romantic indiscretion.

The sight that has impressed me most so far, however, reveals humanity at a more noble level. Early most mornings, a thirtysomething man steps onto his terrace. He typically wears a T-shirt and gym shorts. Draped over his shoulders is a blue-and-white shawl, fringed at both ends. A small plastic box is strapped to his forearm, and another is strapped to the middle of his forehead. The attire must look extremely odd to other early risers who happen to catch sight of him while preparing their morning coffee.

But it's not odd to me. The book of Deuteronomy exhorts us to "love the Lord your God with all your heart, and with all your soul, and with all your might" (6:5). It then instructs us to keep these (and other) divine commands "in your heart" and to teach them to your children, and to think of them "when you lie down and when you rise" (6:7). What's more, "Bind them as a sign on your hand, fix them as an emblem on your forehead" (6:8).

And so, my neighbor and many devout Jews like him throughout the world think of God's words when they wake in the morning and, as instructed, bind to their arms and forehead small, black boxes (tefillin, or phylacteries) containing parchment inscribed with biblical passages, including those just quoted. My neighbor opens what I presume is the Jewish prayer book and utters the same words that every other observant Jew will pray this morning: "I offer thanks before you, living and eternal King, for you have mercifully restored my soul within me; your faithfulness is great."

I say amen to that, my brother and neighbor. I sometimes see him walking to the train station later in the day. He is dressed differently, of course. I don't know what he does for a living or what his day will be like. But chances are, like everyone else he will be bombarded with e-mails, phone calls, meetings, and other distractions. Everyone who calls or e-mails him has an agenda, and their priorities are seldom his priorities. The costly fallout from such a chaotic existence is a world of people who end a workday without even starting to address their first priority. They aren't lazy, not at all, but they lost track of their own priorities while addressing coworkers' requests, fighting fires, and returning messages.

No matter what happens throughout the day, however, for at least a few minutes each morning, my neighbor has reminded himself of his life priorities, and he's unlikely to forget them completely, no matter what the workday may bring.

Remind yourself every day of what you care about and what's ultimately important to you.

Be Accountable: Learn from a Good Boss

I once introduced a new hire to a senior manager. He welcomed her, promised his support, and then said, "Come back to me in a week and answer this question: how will you know you've succeeded this year?"

It was a great question. We usually get up each morning certain of the tasks we have to do all day but considerably less certain about what would constitute doing our work (or life) well over the course of a year. So the new employee thought about her job responsibilities and enumerated the achievements that would constitute a successful year.

That simple process yielded twin benefits: she made herself accountable and she defined success on her own terms. Both are important. First, by articulating the results that would constitute success, she was implicitly making herself accountable not only for her outcomes but also for the decisions and actions she would take to achieve them. And by developing her picture of success, she was defining success on her own terms. Unless we do the same, we risk letting television, the boss, the neighbors, or popular culture define success for us, with hazardous consequences for our well-being. Our media culture projects powerful stereotypes of success, often connected to money, power, beauty, or sexual conquest. Our neighbors often tune in to those cultural cues and gravitate toward acquaintances with the flashiest cars, the biggest McMansions, or the most desirable country-club memberships. In the workplace, our bosses, under pressure from higher-ups, may set entirely unreasonable performance goals for us.

All these external standards have consequences; they often determine who ends up on magazine covers, is invited to neighborhood cocktail parties, or earns promotions and substantial raises. Some of those consequences may seem trivial (like being featured in a magazine), but others are serious (like keeping one's job).

So we can't ignore external standards of success, but deep trouble arises if our sense of self-worth becomes wrapped up in them. We enter an unwinnable rat race as soon as we start living "outside in" by surrendering control of our self-esteem to what others think or say of us. Rather, we need to live "inside out" by setting our own standards of personal success. This book has largely revolved around reclaiming control of our lives in a big, complex, changing world that is largely beyond our control. A powerful tool for reclaiming control is the simple act of developing and being accountable to our own success standards each year, guided by our own vision and purpose.

What's more, accountability involves not only the ability to picture what success would look like but also the willingness to acknowledge when the failure to achieve it is our fault. Today's culture rarely helps instill such accountability. How often, for example, do we hear politicians say, "I'm sorry. I didn't accomplish what I promised, and it was my fault." Politicians know that ideological opponents and media pundits would skewer them for such candor, just as corporate spokespeople know that the words, "We're sorry. We were wrong," invites not forgiveness but costly lawsuits.

Other pitfalls threaten our progress toward appropriate accountability. Other people will sometimes hold us accountable for things beyond our control, like when a sudden economic downturn makes it impossible to deliver a sales quota. And sometimes we are tempted to hold ourselves accountable for what lies beyond our control, like our adolescent child's unfortunate descent into addiction despite a healthy, loving upbringing. Neither an office worker's smoldering anger over being held inappropriately accountable nor a parent's guilt over holding him- or herself inappropriately accountable are going to help them live out their goals and visions. Rather, we have to keep praying for the balance and insight of the earlier-quoted Serenity Prayer: "Give me the courage to change the things I can, the serenity to accept what I cannot change, and the wisdom to know the difference."

Accountability is hard for visionaries because it's challenging to define success this year when pursuing a purpose that transcends a lifetime. The loftier the purpose we commit to pursue, the more difficult it is to picture success. If my purpose is merely to accumulate wealth and status, I can easily judge success: Did my net worth grow? Is my house bigger than my neighbor's? Am I getting ahead of my peers? But if my purpose is to be holy, build the civilization of love, or repair the world, success becomes trickier to measure. Think of the countless nonprofit organizations and for-profit companies that face the same dilemma. Many Jesuit universities and high schools, for example, describe their mission nowadays as "developing men and women for others." A major chemical company aspires "to make this world a better place for our having been in business." Apple Computer proclaims, "We expect to make this world a better place to live."

So how do these organizations measure annual success against these transcendent missions? It's easier for a Jesuit high school to track the percentage of graduates entering college than to figure out how many of these graduates have become men and women for others twenty years later. And it's far easier for Apple to monitor its stock price and tally the number of computers sold each year than to track how much better the world has become because of Apple's efforts. As Albert Einstein once observed, "Not everything that counts can be counted." Sometimes, what counts the most is the hardest to count or measure.

So lots of organizations never even try to assess their success in achieving their highest aspirations. But when they don't, employees begin regarding those aspirations as nothing more than feel-good slogans. In the worst cases, employees become cynical.

It's the same with our individual lives. We can't credibly claim to be living our purpose or values effectively if we can't point to any discernible differences in the way we live, or what we do, or what we accomplish.

What major life priorities do you never seem to tackle? Into what bite-sized pieces could you break those priorities?

What would success look like in your work this week? In your personal life? In your most important relationships?

Fortunately, there's a way forward. I may not be able to judge for sure whether I've been more respectful this year than last, but I can figure out whether I was respectful in the business meeting that just ended.

I usually know when I haven't been respected by a sales clerk, and I also know when I've treated some customer service representative disgracefully because I was angry about a mistake on a bill. The Roman orator Cicero once said, "The best audience for the practice of virtue is one's own conscience."[6] And with my own conscience as audience, I can make myself accountable.

11

Recognize Progress

Use a Spiritual Technology for Purposeful Living

In their best-selling book *Execution*, Ram Charan and Larry Bossidy identified execution as "the great unaddressed issue in the business world today."[1] The same problem afflicts our personal lives. To carry out our goals and live out our values, we need to acquire an execution mind-set, which we've already associated with five characteristics: (1) focus, (2) get real-time feedback that enables real-time course corrections, (3) break major goals into more manageable ones, (4) remind yourself every day what's important, and (5) be accountable.

But how do we incorporate those lessons into real life? How do we transform them into something beyond yet another list to remember during our already preoccupied days? If I could remember what I had to do in the first place, I wouldn't need the five reminders, which quickly become just five more things to forget.

What we need is a habit that will enable us to sew these qualities seamlessly into the fabric of daily life, and that habit has existed in fact for nearly five centuries. Ignatius of Loyola called it the "examen," a Latin word that can mean a test or exam but that also refers to the process of weighing something. Ignatius's examen, then, would connote both examining one's inner thoughts and taking the measure of one's inner feelings.

The essence of the examen is presented in three simple steps (and a more elaborate version follows later). For a few quiet minutes, three times each day,

1. Be grateful.

2. Recall a key objective.

3. Mentally relive your past few hours to draw some lesson learned that might help in the next few hours.

The following excerpts from the *Spiritual Exercises* detail one form of this examen in Ignatius's own words:

> *The First Point* is to give thanks to God our Lord for the benefits I have received.
>
> *The Second* is to ask grace to know my sins and rid myself of them.
>
> *The Third* is to ask an account of my soul from the hour of rising to the present examen, hour by hour or period by period; first as to thoughts, then words, then deeds. . . .
>
> *The Fourth* is to ask pardon of God our Lord for my faults.
>
> *The Fifth* is to resolve, with [God's] grace, to amend them. Close with an Our Father. (#43)

We could expand the key steps of this best practice:

- Place yourself in the presence of God or the Higher Power, or by some other contemplative means, step back from the daily flux of events.

- Pray for (or seek) enlightenment and wisdom.

- Be grateful! You have so much; don't take it for granted. Focus for a moment on what you already have rather than on what you want.

- Mentally scroll through the past few hours to draw lessons learned from the day so far. You might think about your near- or long-term goals, or about some characteristic weakness that hobbles your effectiveness. Pay attention to what you've been thinking and feeling, not just to what you've been doing. If you're a religious believer, consider how God may have been present to you in the events and conversations that have unfolded so far this day. Recall Rabbi Lawrence Kushner's definition of holiness as "being aware that you are in the presence of God."

- Be honest with yourself. If you've not been executing your plan or living the values you aspire to, acknowledge that.

- Finish with hopeful resolution for the future. Be thankful for the opportunity to have recollected yourself, taken stock, and reoriented your thoughts or actions as necessary. And as you have extracted lessons from the past, put the past behind you and look forward.

Just as Walmart executives track real-time sales data to enable immediate course corrections, the examen spotlights personal performance problems before they mushroom into crises. Just as AA members learn to live one day at a time, the examen breaks ambitious life goals and values into manageable daily chunks. Just as that boss asked a subordinate how she would know she succeeded, the examen likewise entails accountability for our thoughts and actions. Finally, like my neighbor's morning prayers, the examen's discipline—including expressing gratitude for blessings received—reminds us of what's important in life.

The genius of this simple practice becomes even more apparent when we consider its origins. When the Jesuits were founded, most religious orders were monastic in character. Monks gathered in chapel multiple times daily to pray as a community. Jesuits broke radically—and controversially at the time—from this monastic regimen to accommodate activist occupations that wouldn't allow assembly for prayer multiple times each day. (Most schools wouldn't run very well, for example, if the faculty and staff all simultaneously disappeared a few times daily!)

But sixteenth-century Ignatius had a great insight that we in the twenty-first century overlook: you and I can choose not to retreat to chapel multiple times daily, but still we need to find ways to keep ourselves focused and recollected as we bob along on the tide of e-mail, phone calls, tasks, and meetings. The examen ingeniously addresses this challenge.

Outdoing Twenty-First-Century Strategists

In fact, Ignatius's sixteenth-century examen uncannily foreshadows (and in some ways goes beyond) highly regarded execution tools of today. The Harvard Business Essentials guide *Strategy*, for example, promotes an examenlike process called a "Model for Staying on Course." Its author summarizes the same sort of challenge that Ignatius was addressing: "No action plan can foresee the many obstacles and changing conditions that people will face over the weeks and months it takes to implement a strategy."[2]

Both Ignatius and this strategy handbook presume that people need to monitor progress against objectives in a world where plans don't survive first contact with the enemy. Both models start by gathering data that will indicate whether things are going well—or poorly. And in both models, we identify key weaknesses and make resolutions for the future.

But with all respect due Harvard's collective wisdom, Ignatius emphasizes vital practices that the business schools miss. For one thing, his examen is a daily habit, which counters the human tendency to slacken vigilance when things appear to be going well— which is exactly when most problems begin snowballing. The authors of *Execution* champion the "relentless pursuit of reality" to counter our natural instinct to want to hear only good news, and the examen's three-times daily discipline epitomizes the "relentless pursuit of reality."[3] What's more, as our radar becomes acute with daily practice, we learn to sense brewing problems before they percolate into plain view—much the way our parents eventually learned to walk into a room and sense that something was wrong before honing in on the broken lamp or unfinished homework.

The more fundamental and consequential difference between the examen and current management tools is that Ignatius invites us to look not just at the workplace but also at our lives and priorities. Instead of focusing only outward through sales reports and conversations with subordinates, the examen also focuses inward for a conversation with ourselves about how the business of life is going. The data include not only our outward behaviors toward others and our work but also what has been going on inside us. We might draw confidence (or consolation) from reflecting on how well we handled a confrontation that would have tripped us up in the past; we might note for the future what exactly we did to defuse the confrontation.

And we might become aware that fear, anger, or envy had been gnawing at us and subtly undermining our performance all morning as we lost patience or lashed out at colleagues. The examen spotlights such feelings, subjects them to conscious scrutiny, explores their cause, and, where possible, puts them aside so they won't derail the rest of our day's performance. In *How Doctors Think*, renowned Harvard Medical School professor Dr. Jerome Groopman points out the sometimes-catastrophic consequences of ignoring our internal data. He recalls a patient "with seemingly endless complaints whose voice sounded to me like a nail scratching a blackboard."[4] After listening to one such complaint and rapidly diagnosing minor gastric trouble, he prescribed antacids and ignored her protests that the problem was persisting. That is, he ignored her until he was paged to the emergency room to find the woman dying of a heart aneurysm.

The lesson he learned has remained with him since: "Emotion can blur a doctor's ability to listen and think. Physicians who dislike their patients" are prone to cut them off, ignore their complaints, or cling to unduly hasty judgments just to avoid the unpleasantness of dealing with them.[5] Most of us don't make life-and-death diagnoses as Groopman does, but all of us deal with family members, bosses, subordinates, or others who may annoy or irritate us. Groopman's insight validates Ignatius's advice to examine ourselves "inside and out." It's important that we monitor our daily performance not just by paying attention to external data (in the doctor's case, lab reports); we need to pay equal attention to internal data, the emotions that might be impeding our effectiveness or even impairing our judgment.

But two even more profound differences separate most business execution models from that of Ignatius. One is gratitude. While most implementation or execution tools focus immediately on problems, Ignatius always insists that we begin with gratitude for blessings. Every examen—and every day—ought to begin with gratitude. That impulse, so often lost in our stressful worldly endeavors, is fundamental to every great spiritual tradition. Here's how the Buddhist monk and author Thich Nhat Hanh expresses it: "Every morning, when we wake up, we have twenty-four brand new hours to live. What a precious gift! We have the capacity to live in a way that these twenty-four hours will bring peace, joy, and happiness to ourselves and others."[6] So, listen to Ignatius of Loyola and Thich Nhat Hanh and be grateful, grateful, grateful. This instinct to gratitude is both spiritual and worldly; researcher Robert Emmons at the University of California–Davis, explains that grateful, optimistic people "cope [better] with daily problems, especially stress, and . . . achieve a positive sense of the self."[7]

The crowning distinction between the examen and other daily updating tools is prayer. The examen is fundamentally a spiritual practice, a prayerful encounter yielding insights that may, in some inscrutable way, bear God's fingerprint. The examen begins with prayer, which frames each day's challenges and frustrations within a broader perspective: this is ultimately not your world but God's. And with that perspective in place, inner calm follows frequently enough.

Even if no other insight dawns during the subsequent few minutes of examen, that renewed perspective makes it time well spent.

The examen likewise ends with prayerful resolution to do better, which brings closure and propels us back into the world. Thus, the examen's simple yet ingenious architecture ensures a healthy balance. On the one hand, the examen demands introspection in a modern culture that shuns the instinct to stop, look inside, and learn from our experience. On the other hand, the examen counteracts the excessive self-absorption that mires us in our own heads. The closing, prayerful resolution to do better prevents us from dwelling unproductively on the past; we've reflected on it, atoned for it if appropriate, and now look forward optimistically and energetically. The model reflects the mind-set eloquently described by the Christian apostle Paul: "Forgetting what lies behind and straining forward to what lies ahead, I press on toward the goal" (Philippians 3:13–14).

Even while our examen reaps insights from our past to improve our future, it teaches us, above all, to live in the present. Our days typically unfurl in frenzied preoccupation with the next meeting to attend, errands to be done, dinner to be prepared, and a hundred other tasks that crowd an efficient day. The monk Thich Nhat Hanh points out that we humans are great at planning and willing to sacrifice today to save for cars and houses tomorrow, "But we have difficulty remembering that we are alive in the present moment, the only moment there is for us to be alive." So he exhorts us to the Buddhist practice of mindfulness, being fully and consciously aware (or mindful) of the present moment. The examen, by briefly pulling us out of our daily maelstrom, can help reorient us to the present. When we get it right, as Thich Nhat Hanh puts it, "Every breath we take, every step we make, can be filled with peace, joy, and serenity."[8]

Learn from the past; envision the future; live in the present. It's a challenging life model to master, but the examen helps us do so.

What are three things you are grateful for this day?

As you go about each day's affairs and conversations, how mindful are you of the present moment, as opposed to preoccupied about the past or the future?

Spiritual Traditions Studded with Execution Tools

The examen's genius is not its sophistication but, conversely, its intuitive simplicity. Many of us have invented similar routines. An acquaintance once observed that the examen's emphasis on gratefulness validated a dinner-table practice from her youth that she now continues with her own children. Over dinner each evening, every family member talks about a "proud-of"—that is, each relates something that went well during the day or some personal behavior he or she is proud of. Through their proud-ofs, this family reflects on the day and expresses gratitude for what transpired.

Another friend relates the examen to a story told about the famed nineteenth-century Jewish philanthropist Sir Moses Montefiore (Montefiore hospitals in various cities honor his legacy). It's told that Montefiore had a cuckoo clock and took the mechanized cuckoo's hourly chirp as a reminder: "What have you done with your life this last hour?" (I admire Montefiore's steadfast conscientiousness, but I probably wouldn't have lasted a week before hurling my shoe at the cuckoo.)

Time-telling technology has evolved significantly since Montefiore's day, and a business-owner friend recommends a variation on the same theme. I was sitting beside him at a conference and heard the alarm on his digital wristwatch. A reminder to order lunch or check in on the stock market with his broker? No, this businessperson's daily alarm reminded him to do his examen.

By incorporating a spiritual examen into his worldly day, he's integrating spiritual practices into everyday life and finding literal, tangible ways to connect faith to work. We spiritual people and religious believers won't live whole lives unless we find ways to do this. And our lives won't feel truly meaningful unless the ideas and beliefs that are of utmost importance to us infiltrate our daily lives.

Numerous religious and spiritual practices take on new meaning and vibrancy when understood as daily tools for the strategy of living well. I once read of a city taxi driver who dangles his Muslim prayer beads from the rearview mirror of his car. Whenever another driver cuts him off, he instinctively reaches for the beads. That simple gesture, he reported, wards off anger and calms him down.

Jakarta, Indonesia, shelters nearly three times the population of New York City and somehow shuttles folks around without a subway system. The unimaginable frustrations of piloting a bus through Jakarta's rush-hour chaos inspired one bus driver to develop his own spiritual self-management system. He put a small box on his dashboard, into which he deposited a penny whenever anger or foul thoughts welled up within him. The technique worked: he collected forty-nine pennies his first day but only sixteen a week later. It was a small price to pay for a regular reminder of the kind of person he aspired to be, and far more valuable than the few coins he accumulated was the greater peace of mind and personal satisfaction he earned in the process.

New York City's transit system tours not only diverse neighborhoods but diverse spiritual execution technologies as well. You ride subway cars alongside Jewish New Yorkers wearing yarmulkes, while Muslim neighbors finger prayer beads, and Catholics pray their rosaries. Bibles and prayer books are yanked out of briefcases. We categorize these as religious devotions, as indeed they are. But consider their power as execution tools: Jews donning yarmulkes, for example, enjoy a very practical, daily opportunity to remind themselves of a core strategic value: to respect God.

In Jesuit lore we find the story of a sixteenth-century brother who invented his own technique for staying focused in a distracting

world. This elderly Jesuit was the community doorkeeper, charged
with receiving beggars, delivery people, visitors seeking counsel,
and whoever else would rap at a rectory door in endlessly annoying succession. So the brother concocted a mental routine to avoid
resenting these many visitors. Upon hearing a knock at the door he
would whisper to himself, "I'm coming, Lord Jesus." Just imagine
what kind of customer service that brother was delivering! Perhaps
he considered this a gesture of pious devotion, but it was a clever
way to remind himself constantly of what was important to him.

Many traditional devotions and spiritual practices might become
equally valuable when rediscovered with this mind-set. Traditional
devotions long since abandoned as old fashioned might once again
be reclaimed as exciting new strategic initiatives. Catholics, for example, once typically blessed themselves with the sign of the cross
whenever they passed a church—which could become comical on
a bus ride through immigrant-heavy neighborhoods where the bus
rolled in rapid succession past the Italian church, then the Polish,
and so on.

A gesture that is repeated constantly but with no conscious
attention can quickly degenerate into an empty habit or, worse,
superstition. But if undertaken with greater presence of mind, these
same gestures of reverence start to yield fruit. We briefly remind
ourselves of our most important concerns in life before succumbing
to the endless stream of quotidian preoccupations that swarm our
consciousness, like where to have lunch, which pitcher a favored
baseball team should acquire, or why the boss is an idiot.

It's becoming ever more crucial to lift ourselves above these
day-to-day distractions, because the e-mail, meetings, and cell-
phone calls are coming more frequently than knocks on that Jesuit
brother's rectory door. And the messages conveyed typically con-
tradict rather than reinforce the impulse to great purpose and high-
minded values. Researchers estimate, for example, that the average
city dweller "is exposed to [five thousand] ads per day."[9] It's a safe
bet that those ads are exhorting us to buy more junk for ourselves
rather than build the civilization of love.

In California's Silicon Valley, where commercialism's omnipresent bleat is amplified by cell phones, pagers, instant messages, and the other gadgetry of this technological wonderland, Ateka's spiritual practices help her cope. Like many devout Muslims, she prays five times daily—at dawn, noon, midafternoon, sunset, and nightfall. The precisely choreographed ritual of Muslim prayer incorporates both mind and body, so if the mind is wandering, the physical gesture of bowing might pull one's attention back to the matter at hand. Some Muslims can routinely make it to a nearby mosque for these prayers, but many others end up praying in fields, factories, or wherever else their daily routine takes them. Ateka, like many of us, occasionally spends some part of an afternoon wandering through shopping malls that invariably, unceasingly, and insistently drum home a consistent set of themes: Take advantage of this sale right now! Buy this blouse and look sexier! But Ateka's spiritual practices regularly remind her that life is ultimately about something more profound than buying more and more stuff. She has more than once found herself retreating to a department store dressing room as noon draws near, not heavily laden with garments to try on, but merely seeking a private place to kneel and worship God. In cubicles on either side of her, clothes hangers clatter as skirts and dresses are slipped on and off, but quiet worship prevails for a few moments in Ateka's fitting room.

Of course, prayer is not magic. Ateka struggles with the same challenges we all face when we're tired, preoccupied, and juggling different tasks. She's honest enough to admit what we all sometimes feel, that "it's hard to focus when you have a lot going on in the day." And dawn prayers can come early when you're an often-exhausted mother of a young child and working outside the house in a demanding profession. On some winter mornings she struggles from a warm bed to a cold floor. "I find myself mumbling through [my dawn prayers] just so I can finish and run back to bed," she says. "Even with five daily prescribed prayers, a Muslim can feel hollow. Perhaps it's how much thought you put into prayer."

I suspect she's being too modest and too scrupulous in wishing that she could be more attentive during prayer at 4:30 a.m. after tending all night to her sick son, or when her mind begins wandering to the many tasks that lie ahead of her at work. For it's precisely then, when we risk complete submersion in daily life's distractions, that a habit of prayer keeps our heads above the surface and our gazes fixed on what we ultimately care about—as she puts it, "completely devoting both our mental and physical selves to worship God."

If prayer is sometimes difficult on wintry mornings, at many other moments it comes easily. The Muslim prayer cycle is a series of moments when, Ateka says, "we completely devote our mental and physical selves to God . . . [in] an exclusive audience alone with God at an appointment given by him." And sometimes it's a pleasure for her to keep that appointment. "If things are going fine, I occasionally try just to bow my head on the floor and thank God for all the bounties." She gets to do so five times a day. Here are some of the words she prays,

> O God, O the One and Only, O the Ever Present,
> O the immensely Generous . . .
> O the One Who Provides all sustenance . . .
> O the Beneficent, O the Merciful,
> O the Matchless Creator of the skies and the earth . . .

I've sometimes driven into New York's LaGuardia Airport, my mind ping-ponging with traveler's preoccupations—do I have my ticket, will I be on time, have I packed what's needed, am I prepared for my talk, and are all the arrangements made? LaGuardia's mazelike ramp network skirts a large parking lot where some hundred or more idle taxis wait their turn to pick up passengers. At certain times of day, I might see a knot of Muslim cabbies at the parking lot's perimeter. Their small prayer rugs are spread on the greasy pavement. Somehow the cabbies ignore diesel fumes, racing engines, and bleating horns. They briefly stop worrying whether they will earn enough today to pay their rent tomorrow. Instead, they pray, as Muslim ritual dictates, that there is no god but God. They prostrate themselves before that one God, touching their foreheads to the ground in reverence.

That gesture reminds them of what's important in their lives, and seeing them at prayer reminds me of what's important in mine. I momentarily forget my worries about tickets and schedules and appointments. I pray, too, perhaps recalling that today, like so many other days, I've forgotten to do the examen that I so frequently recommend to others. I resolve to do better tomorrow. On some tomorrows I do better, but on many tomorrows I don't.

No matter. Every day still brings, as Thich Nhat Hanh puts it, "twenty-four brand new hours to live. What a precious gift!" New opportunities will dawn, and new challenges will arise. As I make my way through them, I will try to learn from my past, live in my present, and look forward to my future.

What are two five-minute blocks of time each day during which you could do a practice like the examen?

What other spiritual technologies or practices do you have that remind you every day of what you think is most important in life?

Let Gratitude and Optimism
Move You Forward

The opening argument for this book's strategy drew on the big picture: we are living in a massively scaled, rapidly changing, complex, and multicultural world. We need a strategy to thrive in such an environment.

The closing case for this book's strategy draws from a very small picture: a snapshot from my years as a Jesuit seminarian.

After finishing college and graduate school, I was assigned to live in one of the United States' largest Jesuit communities, a hundred-strong household populated by saints, scholars, and eccentrics (often enough, all three descriptions fit the same person). The cast of characters included a sixtysomething priest that we might call "Free-Dog," a vague approximation of his nickname. Free-Dog, who had supposedly descended into premature but benign semilunacy, managed minor administrative matters within the community.

Free-Dog would make daily rounds of recreation and mailrooms, pushing around a cart stacked with office or cleaning supplies and providing running editorial commentary about the Jesuit colleagues who crossed his radar. He broadcast at such a high decibel level that anyone within a fifteen-yard radius could tune in to the analysis. Many community members were university professors, and Free-Dog wasn't much impressed by publications in prestigious journals or invitations to address academic conferences; he took particular delight in skewering these intellectual giants and cutting them down to size. Was he really nuts? Hard to say. He often said what the rest of us were thinking but wouldn't dare utter in public. But because Free-Dog was supposedly a lunatic, he got away with it. Not a bad strategy.

A few weeks before I joined Free-Dog's community, I had been awarded a couple of minor academic distinctions at my university commencement. That was all Free-Dog needed to know about me. Forever after, when he saw me coming down the hallway, he would frequently announce with theatrical flair, "Hey, here comes Crissy Fraud," that is, here comes Chris, who thinks he's smart because he won some small-potatoes award at his college graduation. The greeting invariably cheered rather than rankled me. If Free-Dog was needling you, he probably liked you. The folks who really had to worry were those who didn't rate in his commentary at all.

I recalled the anecdote more than once over the months of writing this book. To be sure, I never felt like a fraud while writing, but I was keenly aware that I'm a less worthy messenger of its ideals than those profiled in its pages or countless others I could have included.

A chapter extolled the value of integrity, profiling Johnson & Johnson executives whose countrywide Tylenol recall set their company back some $100 million (back when $100 million was a lot of money). They stood up for their corporate values when compromising those values would have been easier and far less costly. Yet as I was writing about their integrity, I cringed to recall moments in my own corporate climb when the expediency of going along to get along won out over speaking truth to power.

Another chapter counseled freedom from disordered attachments when contemplating major decisions. We sometimes make lousy decisions in business or personal life not because we lack the facts or the intelligence to evaluate them, but because ambition, greed, or a dozen other private demons subtly cloud our better judgment. If I had heeded my own advice over the years, I might have better navigated my one or two (or few dozen) decisions that have been steered less by free pursuit of my life purpose than by pride, fear, or—let's not forget—lust.

Most fundamentally, this book has championed purpose beyond self. Think of Nanette Schorr lavishing her legal expertise on impoverished South Bronx mothers whose children have been placed in protective custody; through that often-frustrating work, Nanette is fulfilling her life purpose, which is to repair the world. Or picture Sr. Saturnina walking up and down the hills of a Caracas slum to teach children to read. Her example locked into focus the sometimes-obscure vision that is God's kingdom. It's not out there in the ethereal distance, over a mountaintop and beyond our lifetimes. Rather, as she put it, "se hace presente"—it's making itself present; it's here. Yes, it's fully alive as she helps children "to live with the dignity that corresponds to children of God's kingdom."

Like Sr. Saturnina, Nanette, and others profiled in these pages, I, too, aspire to a mighty purpose. My reading of my Christian tradition convinces me that I am here on earth to love and serve my neighbors. Yet my implementation of that lofty purpose leaves much to be desired as I reel through an often self-absorbed life more serving of self than serving of neighbor.

And so, as I polished this book's chapters, I sometimes felt a very unpolished vessel for its message. At worst, I felt almost like, well, Crissy Fraud. Who am I to peddle a strategy for living that I haven't perfected in my own life? The Christian apostle Paul summarized succinctly and well what often seems to be my life predicament: "I do not understand my own actions. For I do not do what I want, but I do the very thing I hate" (Romans 7:15). Amen, brother Paul.

But my gnawing disquiet evaporated as I realized that my own quite-flawed humanity doesn't invalidate this book's strategy, but powerfully vindicates it. Indeed, my own shortcomings are the last, best argument for what this book advocates, and my frequently self-absorbed lurch through a confused and confusing world only underscores this book's central case: life is complex, massively scaled, and fast changing; we humans are innately weak, needy, prone to distraction and easily tempted off course. Marry our frailty to the vexing environment in which we live and work, and living well becomes as challenging as assembling the pieces of a vast, complicated puzzle.

But even that isn't the best image. If it were only as simple as fitting puzzle pieces into a big picture, we would eventually complete the task. Rather, life more often feels like a puzzle in which some pieces are suddenly removed and new, unfamiliar ones dropped onto the pile. If the apostle Paul confesses that it was hard for him to stay on track, notwithstanding God's lightning-bolt intervention, of course the rest of us will struggle to make our way through the maze of present-day challenges. No wonder we sometimes become confused, frustrated, discouraged, angry, lost, or overwhelmed and end up, as Paul says, doing the things we hate.

So, how should we respond to the human predicament? We will either lead proactively or live passively, either take charge where we can or drift reactively on the tide of life's vicissitudes, either think hard about what our earthly journey is supposed to mean or try hard to avoid thinking about it.

This book is for those who opt for leadership and are willing to pursue a proactive, deliberately plotted approach to their most important business, the business of their own lives. That means starting with big-picture questions like why we are here on earth and systematically progressing through the nitty-gritty concerns of performing more effectively this very afternoon. We charted a three-part strategy for doing so: live for a mighty purpose, choose wisely, and make every day count. By threading an unchanging purpose and values through your ever-changing circumstances and major decisions, you will weave a life project that holds together as a unified tapestry. Work and home life will tie together, as will religious beliefs and everyday affairs.

Still, no strategy will succeed without courage, a deep-in-the-bones commitment to turn from what is destructive, false, or life sapping because we have glimpsed what is constructive, true, or life giving. And so we return to the unlikely warranty featured in this book's introductory chapter: "Most how-to books guarantee a result if only you read the book; this book guarantees no result if all you do is read it." Our strategy will work, but only when transformed people devote courage, commitment, and will to it.

This book can't bring its strategy alive in another person's heart, but we can at least model the advice of an early guidebook to the Spiritual Exercises and "point, as with a finger, to the vein in the mine and let each one dig for himself."[1] And so, as you dig for renewed commitment and courage, start your excavation with gratitude and optimism.

Let Gratitude Catapult You Forward

Nikki Giovanni reminds us in one poem that "we are better than we think and not quite what we want to be."[2]

We can invigorate our approach to life by pondering both parts of what we might call Giovannni's axiom. First, we're better than we think we are. Second, we are not quite what we want to be or can be: we have more potential than we imagine.

The knowledge that we are better than we think we are ought to spark not arrogance but humble gratitude. Recall the employees of Catholic Health Initiatives who stand for the value of reverence and define it as "profound respect and awe for all of creation." As we race through our lives to catch the next train or squeeze in one more errand, we ought to pause occasionally, look around, and be awestruck by this marvelous world we are racing through.

The Buddhist monk Thich Nhat Hanh exhorted us to remind ourselves daily of the simple but profound blessing that we are alive in this marvelous world: "Every morning, when we wake up, we have twenty-four brand-new hours to live. What a precious gift!"

And Ignatius of Loyola reminded us that we ourselves are one of this world's greatest marvels. Look at the world with gratitude and awe, but look at yourself with the very same attitude. We are more talented, gifted, and resourceful than we ever take time to consider. In one spiritual exercise, Ignatius counsels us to bask gratefully in the sheer wonder of our being by considering "how God dwells . . . also in myself, giving me existence, life, sensation, and intelligence; and, even further, making me his temple, since I am created as a likeness and image of the Divine Majesty" (#235).

Be grateful. Be grateful for your talents and gifts because they are the raw material out of which you will conceive and shape your life's purpose. Whoever we are, whatever our circumstances, we can, as Archbishop Óscar Romero once put it, "do something and do it very well," whether that is raising children, teaching them to read, keeping the streets safe for them, creating dignified jobs for their parents, erecting buildings that will safely shelter them, or thinking and praying benevolent thoughts for their future.

Be grateful because gratitude is what energizes and motivates us to pursue great purpose. As Ignatius, says, we each ought to "ask for interior knowledge of all the great good [we] have received, in order that, stirred to profound gratitude, [we] may become able to love and serve" (#233).

Lead with Optimism
toward a Better World

Gratitude ushers in the optimism that we are capable of being more and better than we are today. We are not quite what we want to be—yet. But we can and will get there. It's worth pondering the fact that Giovanni delivered that poem some twenty-four hours after a deranged gunman had slain more than thirty students and staff at her university campus in the most horrific massacre ever of its kind. At such a moment, above all moments, we need to find the heart and voice to believe that we are better than we think we are.

All of us have been beaten down, disappointed, or hurt by the malfeasance of others, and we stumble, fail, and sin through our own poor choices. The optimistic are convinced that there are grace, mercy, second chances, and forgiveness in this world; we will stand up again and walk forward. And when we don't have the strength to stand up and walk on our own, others will reach out to lift and steady us.

We are bundles of needs, wants, and desires. The optimistic among us believe that our desires and wants need not be enslaved by whatever unhealthy attachment currently preoccupies us or whatever shallow promise an advertiser might thrust in front of us. Rather, we can direct our desires toward some purpose greater than ourselves. We are capable of great vision and don't have to surrender to shortsightedness. We are capable of transcending ourselves, and we don't have to settle for some meager purpose that doesn't uplift us.

The struggle before us is to lead ourselves and our civilization to higher purpose, transcending the small-spiritedness typified in a recent U.S. presidential candidate's damning observation, "Politicians operate on the basis that this generation is too greedy to do anything for the next generation."[3] I can't judge whether this prominent figure has judged himself and his politician colleagues accurately, but I categorically reject his jaundiced judgment on the rest of us.

Politicians and the media may occasionally pander to some greedy, fearful, narrow-mindedness within us. But meanwhile, out here in the real world, legions of the great spirited are doing plenty for the next generation, loving and teaching our kids, sacrificing so they will be well educated, accompanying them through unexpected illness, and preparing a more beautiful and more interesting world for them by what we make, sell, or do. Indeed, if I started chronicling every example of such human goodness in even one small city, I would never finish the task; as the evangelist John wrote, "the world itself could not contain the books that would be written" (John 21:25).

We everyday visionaries are capable of leading civilization forward, no matter that we feel too human, too fragile, too distracted, too greedy, and too everything else for the task. Let's accept the privilege and burden of leading ourselves, our loved ones, and our civilization, whatever our livelihoods and however modest our circumstances. With a clear strategy and the courage of our convictions, we can embrace great purpose, make good choices, and get things done every day of our complicated lives.

The time for the civilization of self is over. Let's start building the civilization of love.

Notes

Introduction

1. David W. Moore and Frank Newport, "People in the World Mostly Satisfied with Their Personal Lives," Gallup News Service, June 20, 1995, quoted in David Whitman, *The Optimism Gap: The I'm OK, They're Not Syndrome and the Myth of American Decline* (New York: Walker and Company, 1998), 3.

2. Quoted in Lawrence J. Lad and David Luechauer, "On the Path to Servant Leadership," in *Insights on Leadership: Service, Stewardship, Spirit, and Servant-leadership*, ed. Larry C. Spears (New York: John Wiley & Sons, 1998), 54.

Chapter 1

1. Conrad de Aenlle, "History Offers Hope and Fear for Kodak," *New York Times*, February 17, 2007.

2. "The World's Largest Corporations," *Fortune*, vol. 158, no. 2, July 21, 2008, p. 165.

3. Charles H. Duell, quoted in Henry Ehrlich, *The Wiley Book of Business Quotations* (New York: John Wiley & Sons, 1998), 190.

4. In 1800, four out of five people were self-employed. *Co-creation and Capitalism: John Paul II's Laborem Exercens*, ed. John W. Houck and Oliver F. Williams (Washington, D.C.: University Press of America, 1983).

5. See, for example, Wei Jiang and Sheena Iyengar research, Columbia University, in Barry Schwartz, Hazel Rose Markus, and Alana Conner Snibbe, "Is Freedom Just Another Word for Many Things to Buy?" *New York Times Magazine*, February 26, 2006, 15.

Chapter 2

1. Laura M. Holson, "From Hollywood to Eternity," *New York Times*, May 20, 2007.

2. Michael E. Porter, *Competitive Strategy: Techniques for Analyzing Industries and Competitors* (New York: Free Press, 1980), xvi.

3. Larry Bossidy and Ram Charan, *Execution: The Discipline of Getting Things Done* (New York: Crown Business, 2002).

4. Aristotle, *Nichomachean Ethics*, trans. Terence Irwin (Indianapolis: Hackett, 1985), 1.2.

5. John Gardner, *On Leadership* (New York: Free Press, 1990), 111.

Chapter 3

1. From Juan Polanco [or Diego Laynez; authorship unknown], "Spiritual Directory of the Mixed Life," in *On Giving the Spiritual Exercises: The Early Jesuit Manuscript Directories and the Official Directory of 1599*, ed. Martin E. Palmer (St. Louis: Institute of Jesuit Sources, 1996), 43.

2. Eamon Duffy, *Saints and Sinners: A History of the Popes* (New Haven, Conn.: Yale University Press, 1997), 48.

3. Andrew Carnegie, *The Gospel of Wealth and Other Timely Essays*, ed. Edward Kirkland (Boston: Belknap Press, 1962), 15–16.

4. Cicero, *Plancio Pro Plancio*, trans. N. H. Watts, Loeb Classical Series, vol. 2 (Cambridge: Harvard University Press, 1977), 80.

5. Carnegie, *Gospel of Wealth*, 16.

6. Robert E. Lane, *The Loss of Happiness in Market Democracies* (New Haven, Conn.: Yale University Press), 5, 19–21.

7. See Robert D. Putnam, *Bowling Alone: The Collapse and Revival of American Community* (New York: Simon and Schuster, 2000), 25, 139–140, 467n26, appendix 1.

8. Findings from a Hudson Institute study; Frank I. Luntz, "Americans Talk about the American Dream," in *The New Promise of American Life*, ed. Lamar Alexander and Chester E. Finn Jr. (Indianapolis: Hudson Institute, 1995), 54.

9. Whitman, *Optimism Gap*, 35, 145n22.

10. Roy C. Smith [former Goldman Sachs partner], quoted in "The Chatter," *New York Times*, January 2, 2005.

11. Gary Rivlin, "If You Can Make It in Silicon Valley, You Can Make It . . . in Silicon Valley Again," *New York Times Magazine*, June 5, 2005.

12. Rabbi Meir, *Talmud*, Sabbath 25b, quoted in Larry Kahaner, *Values, Prosperity and the Talmud: Business Lessons from the Ancient Rabbis*, (New York: John Wiley & Sons, 2003), 1.

13. Alexis de Tocqueville, *Democracy in America*, 12th ed., ed. J. P. Mayer, trans. George Lawrence (New York: Harper Perennial, 1969), 283.

14. Louis Uchitelle, "Were the Good Old Days That Good?" *New York Times*, July 3, 2005.

15. Juliet B. Schor, *The Overworked American: The Unexpected Decline of Leisure* (New York: Basic Books), 109.

16. Toni Bentley, "Nip and Tuck," review of *Beauty Junkies*, by Alex Kuczynski, *New York Times*, October 22, 2006.

17. Ruben Navarrette, "All Together Now, Let's Be Rich and Famous," *Detroit Free Press*, January 21, 2007.

18. de Tocqueville, *Democracy in America*, 283.

19. Sara Rimer, "For Girls, It's Be Yourself, and Be Perfect, Too," *New York Times*, April 1, 2007.

20. Jim McDermott, "Love and Ruins in New Orleans: An Interview with James Carter," *America*, March 20, 2006, 18.

Chapter 4

1. Martin Luther King, "I have a dream," speech, August 28, 1963. Found in *A Testament of Hope: The Essential Writings of Martin Luther King, Jr.*, ed. James Melvin Washington (San Francisco: Harper & Row, 1986), 219.

2. Seneca the Younger, quoted in Henry Ehrlich, *The Wiley Book of Business Quotations* (New York: John Wiley & Sons, 1998), 190.

3. John P. Kotter, *Leading Change* (Cambridge, Mass.: Harvard Business School Press, 1996), 26.

4. Moses Maimonides, *Mishneh Torah*, ed. Philip Birnbaum (New York: Hebrew Publishing, 1967), 329.

5. Pope Benedict XVI, *Deus Caritas Est*, sec. 16, http://www.vatican.va/holy_father/benedict_xvi/encyclicals/documents/hf_ben-xvi_enc_20051225_deus-caritas-est_en.html.

6. UNICEF, "State of the World's Children Report for 2005," http://www.unicef.org/sowc05/english/index.html.

7. Sara Rimer, "The High School Kinship of Cristal and Queen," *New York Times*, June 24, 2007.

8. Loren Eiseley, *The Star Thrower* (New York: Harcourt, 1979).

9. Peter Senge, *The Fifth Discipline: The Art and Practice of the Learning Organization* (New York: Doubleday, 2006), 142.

10. J. M. Velaz, *Pedagogy of Joy*.

11. Henry David Thoreau, letter to Harrison Blake (at Worcester), March 27, 1848, in *The Writings of Henry David Thoreau*, ed. F. B. Sanborn, 160–164 (New York: Houghton Mifflin, 1906), 6:163.

12. Lewis Casson, introduction to *Man and Superman: A Comedy and a Philosophy*, by George Bernard Shaw, xxv (New York: The Heritage Press, 1962).

13. Pope Paul VI, "If You Want Peace, Defend Life," 1977 World Day of Peace message, http://www.vatican.va/holy_father/paul_vi/messages/peace/documents/hf_p-vi_mes_19761208_x-world-day-for-peace-en.html.

Chapter 5

1. Shakespeare, *Macbeth*, act 5, scene 5, lines 26–28.

2. Lawrence Kushner and David Mamet, *Five Cities of Refuge: Weekly Reflections on Genesis, Exodus, Leviticus, Numbers, and Deuteronomy* (New York: Schocken Books, 2003), 93.

3. Kushner and Mamet, *Five Cities of Refuge*, 93.

4. Pierre Teilhard de Chardin, *Hymn of the Universe*, trans. Simon Bartholomew (New York: Harper & Row, 1961), 84.

5. John P. Kotter and James L. Heskett, *Corporate Culture and Performance* (New York: Free Press, 1992), 50.

6. Jim Collins, *Good to Great and the Social Sectors: A Monograph to Accompany "Good to Great"* (Boulder, Colo.: Jim Collins, 2005), 34.

7. James F. Keenan, *The Works of Mercy: The Heart of Catholicism* (New York: Rowman & Littlefield, 2005), xiii.

Chapter 6

1. Bruce Reed, "The Has-Been: Notes from the Political Sidelines," Slate.com, February 7, 2008.

2. Emily Thornton, "Big Guns Aim for Change," *Business Week*, June 24, 2002, 39.

3. *Webster's New World Dictionary, Second College Edition*, s.v. "value."

4. Charlie LeDuff, "For 56 Years, Battling Evils of Hollywood with Prayers," *New York Times*, August 28, 2006.

5. *Webster's*, s.v. "reverence."

6. Lest any suspect Fr. Duffy of being a Trojan horse for heterodox teaching, I would present in his defense no less a luminary of orthodoxy than Pope Pius XII. Fr. Duffy was essentially teaching what the pope proclaimed in the 1943 encyclical *Divino Afflante Spiritu*; see especially secs. 31–38.

7. Augustine, http://gigibeads.net/prayerbeads/saints/augustinehippo.html

8. A teaching of Muhammad quoted in Jamal A. Badawi, "Islamic Teaching and Business," in *Business, Religion, & Spirituality: A New Synthesis*, ed. Oliver F. Williams (Notre Dame: University of Notre Dame Press, 2003), 149.

9. Steven V. Duffy, in *Regis Alumni News* (New York), spring, 2005, 14.

Chapter 7

1. John P. Kotter, "Leading Change: Why Transformation Efforts Fail," *Harvard Business Review* 73, no. 2 (March–April 1995): 59–67.

2. See Kathleen K. Reardon, "Courage as a Skill," *Harvard Business Review* 85, no. 1 (January 2007): 58–64; Bill George, Peter Sims, Andrew N. McLean, and Diana Mayer, "Discovering Your Authentic Leadership," *Harvard Business Review* 85, no. 2 (February 2007), 129–138.

3. Senge, *The Fifth Discipline*, 202.

4. David Kuo, quoted in Peter Steinfels, "The Disillusionment of a Young White House Evangelical," *New York Times*, October 26, 2006.

5. Bill Clinton, comments at funeral of Coretta Scott King, February 7, 2006. A video of President Clinton's remarks can be found at: http://www.youtube.com/watch?v=XNc9IuK0hNc

6. *A Pilgrim's Testament: The Memoirs of St. Ignatius of Loyola*, transcribed by Luis Goncalves da Camara, trans. Parmananda R. Divarkar (St. Louis: Institute of Jesuit Sources, 1995), 12.

7. A *Pilgrim's Testament*, 43.

8. A *Pilgrim's Testament*, 71.

9. Chris Argyris, Warren Bennis, and Robert Thomas, "Crucibles of Leadership," in *Harvard Business Review on Developing Leaders* (Boston: Harvard Business School Press, 2004), 151–152.

10. Collins, *Good to Great*, 36.

11. Abraham Zaleznik, *The Managerial Mystique: Restoring Leadership in Business* (New York: Harper & Row, 1989), 5.

12. Bob Dole, *One Soldier's Story: A Memoir* (New York: HarperCollins, 2005), 175.

13. Dole, *One Soldier's Story*, 264.

14. Walter J. Burghardt, SJ, "Nourishing Head and Heart," *America*, March 20, 2006, 14.

15. Rick Warren, *The Purpose-Driven Live: What on Earth Am I Here For?* (Grand Rapids: Zondervan, 2002), 17.

16. Collins, *Good to Great*, 22, 39.

17. Mother Teresa, *Come Be My Light: The Private Writings of the "Saint of Calcutta,"* ed. Brian Kolodiejchuk (New York: Doubleday, 2007), 149.

Chapter 8

1. James C. Collins and Jerry I. Porras, *Built to Last: Successful Habits of Visionary Companies* (New York: HarperBusiness, 1994), 89.

2. Cardinal John Henry Newman, *An Essay on the Development of Christian Doctrine*, 6th ed. (Notre Dame, Ind.: University of Notre Dame Press, 1989), 40.

3. Abby Ellin, "Under 40, Successful, and Itching for a New Career," *New York Times*, December 16, 2006. The Bureau of Labor Statistics reports that those born from 1957 to 1964, in their first twenty adult years alone, had averaged 9.6 jobs.

4. Richard Luecke, *Decision Making: 5 Steps to Better Results* (Boston: Harvard Business School Press, 2006), 101.

5. Luecke, *Decision Making*, 92.

6. Alden Hayashi, "When to Trust Your Gut," *Harvard Business Review* 79, no. 2 (February 2001), 59–65.

7. Janet Adamy, "How Jim Skinner Flipped McDonald's," *Wall Street Journal*, January 8, 2007.

8. Ben Shpigel, "Two Homes, One Team: Glavine Picks Mets," *New York Times*, December 2, 2006.

9. Malcolm Gladwell, *Blink: The Power of Thinking without Thinking* (New York: Little, Brown, 2005).

10. Walter J. Ciszek, SJ, *With God in Russia*, with Daniel L. Flaherty, SJ (New York: McGraw Hill, 1964), 61.

11. Walter J. Ciszek, SJ, *He Leadeth Me*, with Daniel L. Flaherty, SJ (New York: Image Books, 1975), 88.

12. The proper phrasing of this famed maxim is debated among historians of Jesuit spirituality. For a summary of the debate and further sources, see Chris Lowney, *Heroic Leadership* (Chicago: Loyola Press, 2003), 299.

13. Joseph H. Fichter, SJ, *James Laynez: Jesuit* (St. Louis: B. Herder Book Co., 1944), 77–78.

14. The original version of this prayer is attributed to the Protestant theologian Reinhold Niebuhr (d. 1971) in the 1930s or 1940s; it was later modified and adopted by the AA movement.

15. Kate Zernike and Jeff Zeleny, "Obama in Senate: Star Power, Minor Role," *New York Times*, March 9, 2008.

16. Parker Palmer, *Let Your Life Speak: Listening for the Voice of Vocation* (San Francisco: Jossey-Bass, 2000), 44–47.

17. "Short Directory to the Spiritual Exercises" [1580s], archives of the Belgian Province of Jesuits, in Martin Palmer, *On Giving the Spiritual Exercises: The Early Jesuit Manuscript Directories and the Official Directory of 1599* (St. Louis: Institute of Jesuit Sources, 1996), 205.

18. Henry David Thoreau, "Walden," in *The Works of Henry David Thoreau* (New York: Thomas J. Crowell, 1940), 118.

19. Steve Martin, "The Death of My Father," *The New Yorker*, June 17, 2002, 84.

20. Noel M. Tichy and Warren G. Bennis, *Judgment: How Winning Leaders Make Great Calls* (New York: Penguin, 2007), 1, 32.

21. Thomas Cahill, *Pope John XXIII* (New York: Viking Penguin, 2002), 177.

Chapter 9

1. Quoted in W. R. Forrester, *Christian Vocation: Studies in Faith and Work* (London: Lutterworth Press, 1951), 147–148.

2. Martin Luther, "The Estate of Marriage" (1522), in *Luther's Works*, trans. and ed. Walther I. Brandt (Philadelphia: Muhlenberg Press, 1962), 45:40.

3. John Calvin, "Institutes of the Christian Religion," 3.10.6, *Library of the Christian Classics*, ed. John T. McNeill, trans. Ford Lewis Battles (Philadelphia: Westminster Press, 1960), 20:724.

4. Palmer, *Let Your Life Speak*, 10.

5. Frederick Buechner, *Wishful Thinking: A Theological ABC* (New York: Harper and Row, 1973), 95.

6. Gerard Manley Hopkins, "As Kingfishers Catch Fire," in *The Poetical Works of Gerard Manley Hopkins*, ed. Norman H. MacKenzie (Oxford: Clarendon Press, 1990), 141.

7. Elizabeth Barrett Browning, "Aurora Leigh," 7.821–824, ed. Margaret Reynolds (Athens: Ohio University Press, 1992), 487.

8. Gerard Manley Hopkins, "God's Grandeur," in *The Norton Anthology of English Literature, Revised*, ed. M. H. Abrams (New York: W. W. Norton, 1968), 1433.

9. Kushner and Mamet, *Five Cities of Refuge*, 93.

10. Pope Paul VI, "If You Want Peace."

Chapter 10

1. Liz Robbins, "Defense in Dallas? Coach Has Disciples," *New York Times*, February 19, 2006.

2. Steve Lohr, "Preaching from the Ballmer Pulpit," *New York Times*, January 28, 2007.

3. *The Catholic Encyclopedia: An International Work of Reference on the Constitution, Doctrine, Discipline, and History of the Catholic Church*, s.v. "John Berchmans."

4. Robert Butterworth, quoted in Lisa Belkin, "Resolved: Go Easy on the Resolutions," *New York Times*, December 31, 2006.

5. "Mets Complete First 3-Game Sweep at Home!" *New York Sun*, August 11–13, 2006.

6. Cicero, *Tusculan Disputations*, 2.26. Quoted in Max Stackhouse et al., editors, *On Moral Business: Classical and Contemporary Resources for Ethics in Economic Life* (Grand Rapids: William B. Eerdmans, 1995).

Chapter 11

1. Bossidy and Charan, *Execution*, 5.

2. Luecke, *Strategy*, 96–97.

3. Bossidy and Charan, *Execution*, 30.

4. Jerome Groopman, *How Doctors Think* (Boston: Houghton Mifflin, 2007), 24.

5. Groopman, *How Doctors Think*, 25.

6. Thich Nhat Hanh, *Peace Is Every Step: The Path of Mindfulness in Everyday Life* (New York: Bantam, 1991), 5.

7. Robert Emmons, quoted in Gregg Easterbrook, "Rx for Life: Gratitude," http://www.beliefnet.com/story/51/story_5111.html.

8. Hanh, *Peace Is Every Step*, 5.

9. Walter Kirn, "Here, There, and Everywhere," *New York Times Magazine*, February 11, 2007, 17–18.

Let Gratitude and Optimism Move You Forward

1. The Directory to the Spiritual Exercises of 1599, chapter 8, no. 1, quoted in W. W. Meissner, "Psychological Notes on the Spiritual Exercises," *Woodstock Letters: A Historical Journal of Jesuit Educational and Missionary Activities*, vol. 92, no. 4 (November 1963), 355.

2. Nikki Giovanni, "We Are Virginia Tech," Virginia Tech Convocation, April 17, 2007. This material was used by permission of Nikki Giovanni.

3. Marc Santora, "Potential G.O.P. Contender Tries Out Campaign Lines," *New York Times*, May 6, 2007.

Acknowledgments

I t's my great pleasure to thank some of those who made this book better or encouraged me along the way.

How dreary to read a book's first draft! Let me thank those who did so and offered valuable comments, including Mari Carlesimo, Rev. Jim Connors, SJ, Tom Loarie, Margaret Mathews, Ramon de Oliveira, and Christian Talbot.

A panel of "experts" in the business of everyday life responded to my e-mailed questions and contributed valuable ideas, including Joe Bringman, Dave Hansen, Harry Walters, Joanne Wakim, Kerry Robinson, Vin Maher, Joan Van Hise, Fred Fields, Susan Blansett, Marilynn Force, Dominique Gallego, Mike Henderson, and John Law.

The book tells various stories about everyday heroes who, to their great credit, would be too modest to apply the word *hero* to their lives. I thank all of those who are portrayed in previous pages, some identified by name in the book and others pseudonymously; I am grateful they willingly subjected themselves to the time and annoyance it took to help me get their stories right. I would also like to thank those who helped me find these stories or pull the stories together, particularly Arturo Serrano, Colleen Scanlon, Linda Worley, Maha Elgenaidi, Mike Dahir, George Simon, and Gail.

Now my nephew Colin can read all of these words by himself. He is a great guy, and I am very happy that he is my nephew! Thank you, Colin, for being my friend!

I'm grateful to Jim Fitzgerald, who served as agent for this book. Joe Durepos not only brought this book to Loyola Press but also offered guidance along the way and with good humor bore the brunt of my occasional rants. Vinita Wright edited this book (as well as my first book); she knows (and now readers do) how highly

I trust her judgment and how deeply I value her skills and grasp of language—not only does she have a marvelous ability to make sentences, paragraphs, and chapters better, but she is also a trusted advisor. Similarly, Katherine Faydash added great value in her work on the manuscript. I write this very early in the marketing process, so the Loyola Press marketing staff will forgive that I am not singling them out by name. But I would be remiss in not thanking Michelle Halm, who has been a supportive presence at Loyola Press for some time.

What do I have that was not given to me? I'm grateful for those whose love, hard work, inspiration, friendship, or example is instrumental in whatever I've managed to accomplish in my life. Of the very many that ought to be recognized, I name too few and too briefly, starting with my late father and my mom, Maureen, and Sean and Tony, Annette and Colin; my teachers in grammar and high school; so many Jesuits, living and dead; my high school buddies, the "guys," who turned fifty with me in the year that I write this, and their families; my Morgan and Fordham and many other friends who have remained so in the many years of our respective (and shared) odysseys.

The support of all these folks made this a much better book. Many inadequacies remain; for these, I take full credit.

Beyond the Printed Page . . .

Heroic Living and *Heroic Leadership* by Chris Lowney are now available as eBooks. Visit www.loyolapress.com to purchase these other formats.

Ignatian Spirituality Online . . .

Learn more about prayer, spiritual direction, retreats, and how to make good decisions at www.ignatianspirituality.com